ARCHITECTURE IN THE GARDEN

JAMES VAN SWEDEN

WITH THOMAS CHRISTOPHER

ARCHITECTURE IN THE GARDEN

FOREWORD BY PENELOPE HOBHOUSE

FRANCES LINCOLN

Architecture in the Garden

Frances Lincoln Ltd

4 Torriano Mews

Torriano Avenue

London NW5 2RZ

www.franceslincoln.com

Published in the United States by Random House, Inc., New York,

and simultaneously in Canada by Random House of Canada Limited, Toronto.

www.atrandom.com

British Library Cataloguing-in-Publication data

A catalogue record for this book is available from the British Library.

ISBN 0 7112 2189 8

Printed and bound in Singapore

9 8 7 6 5 4 3 2 1

Book design by Barbara M. Bachman

JAMES VAN SWEDEN IS INTERNATIONALLY ACCLAIMED AS A LANDSCAPE ARCHITECT WHO, WITH HIS partner Wolfgang Oehme, has evolved an entirely new concept in garden design. In the 1980s it was called the "New American" garden, but twenty years later and into the new century, not only has he shaped landscapes throughout the world but the Oehme, van Sweden "look" has fashioned the taste and opinions of a far wider audience who admire his work, read his books, and follow his inspiration. In his contribution to both public and private garden design, from large-scale parks to intimate walled city gardens, his work has become a byword for excellence.

Although van Sweden is primarily considered a landscape architect who works with nature, massing plants in great scrolls to create abstract pictures, his art disguises the basic disciplines and careful manipulation that go into providing the essential framework that forms the bones on which he imposes his pictures. Nothing is left to chance; each design is a carefully orchestrated affair in which basic and classical tenets of garden architecture are the basis. In this book he shares his depth of knowledge with the reader. As he says himself, he wants to make the "secrets of his trade" available, to open the eyes of amateurs as well as professionals to the importance of the man-made elements in a good garden, and, by enlightening, teach how to analyze and appreciate the finer points in any scheme.

This book, however, is not only about theories of proportion, scale, and balance; it is eminently practical as well. By outlining his own approach to the different challenges he has had in his career, he shares a thought process that deliberately dispels some of the mysteries of his trade. By describing situations he has faced and problems he has solved, he not only stimulates further thought but also offers illuminating solutions. Avenues, paths and terraces, fences and steps, and reflecting water and naturalistic ponds are all geared to suit each particular garden. In the country the mores of the "borrowed" landscape can be reflected in the garden scheme, whereas in a town garden it is possible to create a secluded oasis attuned to a search for relaxation, and, most important, to suit the individual client. The setting and topography of a rural site will dictate the atmosphere you wish to create—van Sweden has developed his eye to read a regional landscape and work with it rather than imposing on it. His architectural elements develop the logic of what is already there, to make them fit seamlessly into a scheme and work functionally for an owner. In the small city garden he can study the client's own aesthetics and develop an intimate space in which the style of the house and owner's needs are amalgamated. It seems as if van Sweden has an intuitive gift for assessing a situation, but in this book he explains how this has been developed by a disciplined and logical thought process in which everyone can share. All in all, garden designing is a dialogue between artifice and nature, between the elements that create the essential framework and the softening plants that decorate it. As the book explains and beautifully illustrates, every garden needs an architectural background to hold the design together and ensure that it will mature gracefully.

ACKNOWLEDGMENTS

I AM DEEPLY INDEBTED TO HELEN PRATT, MY LITERARY AGENT, FOR ENVISIONING THE GARDEN book series of which this is the third volume. Helen also introduced me to Jason Epstein, who was editor in chief at Random House when we started. Jason enthusiastically endorsed the series, defined its voice and style, and edited the first two books. He then introduced me to David Ebershoff, publishing director of the Modern Library, who edited this book with contagious enthusiasm and energy. David's contributions to clarity of text are invaluable. He and his team, including Barbara Bachman, the book's designer, have given it great beauty.

Thomas Christopher was a joy to work with on the text. He and I shared animated discussions and lots of good fun while traveling together to see all these gardens anew. Tom captures my voice perfectly.

Others to whom I am indebted for writing are Robin Herbst for her early drafts, Charles Turner for his sage advice and careful attention to details, and Douglas Brenner for suggestions about style.

I thank my partners at Oehme, van Sweden & Associates, Inc.—Wolfgang Oehme, Sheila Brady, Eric Groft, and Lisa Delplace—for their enormous contributions to the design and execution of the many gardens that you will see and learn about. Of course, without their dedication, insights, and willing collaboration, a book of this scope would not be possible.

Ching-Fang Chen produced most of the exquisite drawings, each of which could stand alone as a work of art. Other members of my design staff who have contributed include Christopher Moore and John Wilson.

Debra Gilmore, Judy Sternlight, Martha Turner, and Steel Colony have provided invaluable help in a variety of roles. Richard Felber and Roger Foley are responsible for many of the beautiful photographs.

Finally, I wish to thank all the clients who have made these gardens possible through their commitment to beauty and courage to innovate. I am especially grateful to them for their patience and gracious comments during interviews and for allowing us to revisit and photograph their gardens. Their enthusiasm is a continuing source of inspiration.

CONTENTS

INTRODUCTION

I'VE BEEN DESIGNING AND BUILDING GARDENS FOR THE PAST THIRTY YEARS. ALONG THE WAY I'VE learned that an essential part of gardening is sharing. Sharing seeds or cuttings of favorite plants is, of course, something most gardeners do. Many of the plants in my own gardens came to me with that personal sort of provenance. Even more precious to me, though, have been the skills and insights that other gardeners have shared with me.

That's why I've written this book. I want to let you in on some of the secrets of my trade, the skills and insights I've collected throughout my career. In this way I want to take the mystery out of the garden-making process and show you how to make your own plot functional and beautiful. In particular, I want to open your eyes to the essential role that architecture plays in organizing any landscape. I want to share with you the know-how you will need to give your garden "good bones"—the framework of well-conceived paths and terraces, well-defined and integrated edges, and other man-made features that ensure enduring grace and make a landscape easy to live with.

One of the most important skills for any gardener is knowing how to "read" a garden—how to look with a professional's analytical eye at landscapes you already know well and those you encounter in your travels. That sort of critical thinking has a very practical value. Once you uncover the secrets of proportion and scale, arrangement, texture, and materials, you will understand why those landscapes work or don't work. Applying this knowledge at home, you can begin to design a garden suited to your wishes, needs, and budget.

Through this book, I'll be your companion on walking tours of gardens that I have designed. I'll help you understand the techniques and natural features that make those gardens beautiful. I also want you to learn from my false starts and mistakes—to study not only the projects that worked but also those that did not.

Writing this book has been a learning process for me. Much of what I do in my daily work is intuitive. After all these years, the process has become second nature. In translating it to paper, though, I've had to analyze my own working methods. I've had to tease out the different steps of what is ordinarily a single, ongoing procedure. I've had to reduce each of those steps to its simplest form and then place it in the proper sequence. As a result, what I had intended to be a voyage of discovery for you, the reader, has become very much a joint venture. I hope that you will let me join you in this exploration of garden making.

HOW TO USE THIS BOOK

Art or any craft is part theory and part practice. To create a sound architectural framework for your garden, you must understand some fundamental principles of design. You must also understand how to put these principles into practice. You must know how to express them in wood, stone, and earth.

In the following pages I've used a dual approach to explaining the techniques of garden architecture. After a discussion in Part One of how my architectural style evolved, Part Two, "Garden Studies," comprises a series of succinct chapters, such as "Art Belongs in the Garden" (Chapter 5), "The Country Garden" (Chapter 6), and "The Town Garden" (Chapter 7), in which I've laid out the principles I follow in designing and creating a particular type of outdoor space. To show how I apply these principles, I've followed the introductory text of each chapter with studies of actual gardens. These may be in-depth case studies or briefer cameos. Each garden illustrates the preceding expository text. The focus of all the studies is on practicality. Each one concentrates on techniques and solutions you can actually use in building your own garden.

The natural tendency will be to turn to the section of the book that bears most directly on your situation. The city gardener, for example, will surely be tempted to flip forward to "The Town Garden." That's fine. However, I urge you afterward to turn back to the book's beginning and work your way through the whole of it in sequence. The different parts were designed to work together in providing a well-rounded introduction to garden architecture. They are individual lessons that unite to form a complete curriculum.

That word, *curriculum,* may sound intimidating, but I've worked hard on making this book enjoyable and easy to use. The illustrations and photographs of gardens are the heart of this book. The precisely detailed schematic drawings of outstanding architectural details will furnish all the information you will need to reproduce those works yourself.

Part Three, "Gallery of Architectural Features," is an illustrated glossary of a garden's "built elements." These include the walls, decks, fences, paths, gates, and other man-made features that constitute the basic vocabulary of garden architecture.

Taste is a personal matter and so, for the most part, is gardening. When we begin to change the topography of our lot, however, or start installing architectural features such as fencing, this may bring us under the jurisdiction of local building codes or environmental ordinances. For the most part these regulations are designed to keep gardeners and homeowners from endangering themselves or others, and compliance is fairly straightforward. In some situations, expert advice can be invaluable, especially if you find you need to file for permits or approvals. Do you need this sort of assistance? To find out, consult the Appendix: "Rules and Regulations for Construction," which contains a short checklist of helpful queries.

One final word: Many of the gardens featured in this book represent very considerable commissions

Willem de Kooning (1904–1997), *Door to the River*, 1960. Oil on canvas. 80" x 70". Whitney Museum of American Art, New York; purchase, with funds from the Friends of the Whitney Museum of American Art. © 2002 Willem de Kooning Revocable Trust/Artists Rights Society (ARS), New York.

that were executed on a lavish scale. Don't let that discourage you from examining them closely. You may wonder how such high-end landscapes relate to your needs. In fact, when it comes to planning a comfortable and rewarding garden, the challenges that confront the owner of an estate or a weekend cottage are often substantially the same. The principles and techniques used for organizing a large site work equally well in a more modest setting.

In choosing a model from which to learn, the important point is not to find the work that most closely resembles your own situation. To learn, you need to study the best. As a young man I loved to paint. The works that I took for models then were not those of my fellow art students. Instead, I looked to the paintings of the great masters. Youths always dream, but I didn't really think I would be the next Jan Vermeer or Willem de Kooning. Still, I knew that their canvases had the most to teach. On a humbler level, I believe that you will find much to emulate in the best of thirty years' work by myself and my colleagues at Oehme, van Sweden & Associates.

PART ONE

EVOLUTION OF A STYLE

INSPIRATIONS

chapter one

M Y FATHER WAS A BUILDER. HE BUILT ALL KINDS OF HOUSES, FROM SNUG

suburban bungalows to grand estates on large tracts of land. He loved big cars and big cigars, and he never

defined himself as an artist. Still, in that era before power tools, his relationship with the materials he cut

and shaped by hand was personal; the respect for craftsmanship was an article of faith with him. I remem-

ber an incident from a summer in my teens when I was working for him. He had given me the task of cutting

a door frame's trim. Perhaps I hadn't measured quite accurately; perhaps I hadn't cut quite to the line.

When I nailed the trim in place, there were gaping cracks where the pieces met at the corners. I was hur-

riedly filling these with plastic wood when my father discovered what I was doing. His outrage was unfor-

gettable, and I believe it was only his determination to save his son from himself that prevented my father

from firing me on the spot.

This explains, in part, who I am and why I have always felt a compulsion to build. I never did measure

up to my father's standard as a carpenter, but I certainly inherited the passion he so clearly felt for the act of

building. I too love the process of arranging raw materials into something tangible and useful.

I studied architecture at the University of Michigan, and in my third year was inspired by Professor Stanley Sherman's course on urban design. He assigned the students the task of designing a new town. That expanded my horizons, quite literally, for whereas previously I had been thinking structure by structure, now I began to think of structures in relationship to one another and in relationship to the surrounding landscape. After finishing my undergraduate degree, I went on to graduate work in landscape architecture.

What is the point of looking backward in this fashion? I believe that knowing who you are is essential

I drew this view along a Delft canal in 1960.

when you come to design your garden. I grew up in the expansive midwestern landscape of Grand Rapids, Michigan, and I still love its big sky, rolling meadows, and sweeping spaciousness. That preference is in my genes: my grandparents came to the United States from the Netherlands. After my first year of graduate study, I transferred to the University of Delft. Immediately I felt at home among the open vistas and understated topography of the Netherlands. At the same time, I also found myself drawn irresistibly to the built spaces of the Dutch landscape, the extraordinary town squares of medieval cities such as Delft, Gouda, and Haarlem.

Here I am at age twenty in the Schaddelee garden, Fort Myers, Florida.

Beautifully proportioned and constructed on a friendly human scale, these spaces were concrete examples of the urban centers we had imagined in Professor Sherman's seminar room. These squares were something I had never found in American cities: a living room for the whole community, the central meeting place and pivot for town life. I also recall being struck by how the use of identical materials integrated the outdoor space and surrounding buildings into a single unit.

Influences aren't all just memories of the past. What we see and experience as we move through life can also transform our tastes. That is why I urge would-be designers to visit as many gardens as possible. Analyze each to understand how it makes you feel the way you do. If a particular space feels hospitable or inhospitable, pace off the dimensions, look at how it is enclosed, and determine what materials give it character. Uncover the devices that the garden's maker used, and later you can adopt or avoid them in your own landscape. Sit in the furniture in the gardens you visit. Pretend it's your garden and walk around it as you might in pursuing your business through a typical day. You'll soon get a sense of whether the spaces and their arrangement would fit you. Bring a camera and record architectural details that you find appealing. The photographs can serve as patterns you can later use.

Sometimes what you experience on these visits may have a profound effect on your understanding of what constitutes a garden. My first encounter with the garden of the Villa Lante in Bagnaia, Italy, was a turning

Fountain of the River Gods, Villa Lante, Bagnaia, Italy.

Zen monastery garden of Ryoanji, Kyoto, Japan.

point of that sort. The Villa Lante lies just 40 miles north of Rome. It was built as a country retreat for Cardinal Giovan Francesco Gambara; the design is attributed to Giacomo da Vignola, the man who succeeded Michelangelo as the Vatican's architect. The garden he designed for the cardinal survives more or less intact, though by modern American standards it hardly qualifies as such. You'll find virtually no flowers and little turf. Instead, it is a sculptor's fantasy of carefully balanced masses of masonry—walls, pavilions, and paths—and clipped evergreen hedges. A central cascade of clear water, which drops from terrace to terrace, bursting from fountains, pouring through channels and sweeping out into still pools, serves as the backbone of the composition. The drama, and the fascination, of the garden lies in this contrast—the strict, geometric formality of the built elements and greenery, versus the dynamic formlessness of the water.

An even greater revelation was my first visit to Japan in 1983. Traditional Japanese household architecture, both indoors and out, has taken as its unit of measurement the 3-by-6-foot dimensions of the tatami, the woven rush mat with which the Japanese classically cover their floors. Using this as the basic module not only keeps house and garden at a human scale, it also makes the two function as a single unit.

The Japanese garden makers also excel at expressing a deeply felt naturalism through a spare, fundamentally abstract vision. The most famous example of this is the abbot's garden, a fifteenth-century courtyard in the Zen monastery of Ryoanji in Kyoto. The garden occupies a space about the size of a tennis court, and consists of fifteen stones set in raked white sand. Still, the garden seems to encapsulate vast space, archipelagoes of islands and distant horizons. This is not a garden for strolling—indeed, no one ever steps into it except for the monk who cares for it. Instead, you arrive at the long, darkly polished wooden verandah fronting the abbot's quarters (hojo). Sitting on the edge with the hojo behind you, the harmonious simplicity of the garden sweeps your mind clean and inspires you to contemplate the mysteries of Zen. Turning around, the unexpected beauty of the altar room is startling. At the center it displays a dragon painted on the ceiling and an image of Buddha as the object of veneration.

That is garden architecture of the highest order.

The emotional landscapes of the late Brazilian landscape architect Roberto Burle Marx have also greatly influenced me. He was a man who excelled as a singer, chef, and painter in addition to his accomplishments as a plantsman and designer of landscapes. This astonishing versatility was the secret of his strength as a designer. His love of music, for instance, expressed itself in his lyrical modeling of the free-form architectural elements with which he shaped garden walls and floors. Marx didn't design those structures—he composed them like melodies. He managed color and texture with a painter's confidence, turning every architectural element into a work of art. He laid out the promenades along the Copacabana in Rio de Janeiro in paisley patterns of black, gray, and white basalt. He assembled walls from recycled stone or terra-cotta building ornaments. Others he laid out in sensuous, undulating lines, inlaying them with colorful mosaics. He spread out terraces like carpets of colored stones or even shells and bits of glass.

When I need a bolt of creative energy, I look at the designs of two American landscape architects: Martha Schwartz and Peter Walker. They are true innovators who also have been greatly influenced by paint-

Abbot's quarters,
Zen monastery of
Ryoanji, Kyoto,
Japan.

Dessert table with
painted tablecloth
by Roberto Burle
Marx (1909–1993),
Guaratiba, Brazil.

ing and sculpture. They place unusual materials in bold patterns that always free my thinking and reveal new possibilities. Walker typically uses granite, stainless steel, and glass. Schwartz always surprises me with her use of prosaic, artificial materials such as plastic, AstroTurf, and colored gravel.

Although I savor the differences of all these designers from whom I draw strength, I know that in one respect all their work is the same. Each of their gardens—indeed, any successful garden—is a work based in illusion. A garden is always a sort of visual sleight of hand, a deft manipulation by which the conjurer transforms random nature into an architectural scene that once existed only in his or her mind's eye.

Composer Igor Stravinsky once remarked that natural sounds—bird calls, water falling over stones,

Miami Sound Wall, designed by Martha Schwartz.

Copacabana promenade, Rio de Janeiro.

breezes moving through evergreen branches—are materials for music, but not

the music itself. Architect Charles W. Moore once observed that "to become

music, sounds must be chosen and arranged." He added, "So it is with gar-

dens." The notes of the garden composer are those landscape elements—rocks,

plants, timber, and water—that you arrange to create a view, a picture,

Plaza Tower, Costa Mesa, California, designed by Peter Walker and Partners.

an entire experience. Architecture, like the composer's rhythm and harmony, is what bounds the experience and defines it.

At a fundamental level, all the arts spring from the same creative impulse, and all are connected. Sometimes the connection may not be readily apparent. Music and dance, for example, may not seem at all related to garden making. But consider: Music and dance are both ephemeral, performance arts. So is gardening. Gardens, after all, are always changing, growing or dying, and you must learn to treat them as a process, an activity rather than a static work.

Rhythm—deliberate, measured repetition—is central to music and dance. It's also a key to effective garden architecture, though in the landscape we create rhythm through the spacing and repetition of elements of similar color, texture, and form. The pattern with which stones or bricks are set in a pavement creates an architectural rhythm. That rhythm can be slow and soothing, as in a regular progression of large rectangular flagstones, or it can be lively, a hot, jazzy rhythm like the ones you'll find in Marx's paths of multicolored stone blocks.

Johannes Vermeer (1632–1675), *A Lady at the Virginals with a Gentleman*. Oil on canvas. 29" x 25". The Royal Collection © 2002, Her Majesty Queen Elizabeth II.

Pieter de Hooch (1629–1684), *A Woman Preparing Bread and Butter for a Boy*, about 1660–1663. Oil on canvas. 26 7/8" x 20 7/8". The J. Paul Getty Museum, Los Angeles.

Similarly, it's useful to think in terms of choreography when planning a garden. As we've already noted, a garden is a succession of experiences. The way you lay out architectural elements such as paths and gates will determine the sequence those experiences will take. Essentially, you are planning the footsteps of the visitor, choreographing their visit.

Painting—which deals with light, color, and texture—and sculpture—the manipulation of mass, form, and space—also have an obvious relevance to garden design. During my days as a graduate student in the Netherlands, I became intrigued by the paintings of the seventeenth-century Dutch masters. Years later they continue to enrich my work as a garden architect. I've modeled terraces on the beautifully patterned and proportioned floors I found in the interior scenes of Vermeer and Pieter de Hooch. The way the Dutch old masters handled light, color, and materials in their paintings of courtyards and terraces has profoundly influenced my

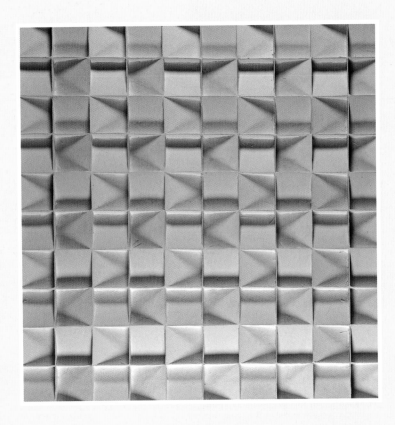

J. J. Schoonhoven
(1924–1994), *Large Relief
of Squares*, 1964.
Cardboard relief.
39" x 39".

designs for walled garden spaces. I've found something very different but equally inspiring in the abstract works of modern Dutch artists: Jan Schoonhoven, Karel Appel, and Anton Heyboer. I'm fascinated by the way that they express exuberance, repose, and even violence in the case of Appel's work, with patterns of color and mass. Just as our interest in a poem or painting or piece of music deepens when we understand the elements underlying its construction, a garden too can become more pleasing as we understand the fundamentals of its architecture.

THE GARDENER'S NEED

FOR ARCHITECTURE

THERE IS A TRUTH ABOUT GARDEN MAKING THAT TOO FEW GARDENERS understand: a collection of plants is just that—a collection. Unless and until that collection is structured and organized in a pleasing and functional manner, it is not and never will be a garden. It's as if you gathered together an assortment of your favorite timbers, stones, and tiles and prematurely declared it a house.

Why do gardeners so often ignore the need for architecture? The reason, I believe, is that for most of us, plants are always at center stage in the garden. It was the luminous hue of a flower, the soft, caressive texture of a leaf, that drew us there in the first place. We become so preoccupied in caring for these charges that we forget that the garden should be more than just a nursery.

As many Americans have moved away from the sterile regimentation of front yard/backyard/foundation planting over the last generation and toward a more natural gardening style, many have mistakenly come to see architecture as part of the problem. Architecture, in this view, is just another artificial tyranny that man

imposes on the landscape. However, if we look closely at those plants that you and I love, we discover a truth. Without a strong architectural foundation, no garden can be truly natural. Nature was the first architect, and she remains an insistent practitioner, instilling architectural order into every aspect of her landscape.

The feather reed grass, *Calamagrostis acutiflora* 'Stricta', (opposite) one of the most graceful of the ornamental grasses, has become something of a signature of my design work. The lush clumps of erect foliage are sculptural, but the plant's real payoff is the flower stems that explode upward in early summer. Each stands as much as 6 feet tall and is far taller relative to its diameter than any steel and stone skyscraper, yet even after the sap drains out and life retreats to the grass's roots in fall, the stems withstand the storms and snows of winter to meet the spring still upright.

That's architecture of the highest order, and you find it everywhere in nature. You find it in the precise geometry of the alpine plants that fill rock gardens: the leaves and stems packed so as to minimize the impact of cold, wind, and intense high-mountain light. You find architecture in the meticulous arrangement of a cactus's spines, which have evolved not only to ward off hungry grazers but also to condense and collect night's dew and then deposit it, drip by drip, onto the root zone right around the plant.

On a more practical level you also find models in nature for all the common features of landscape architecture. I remember becoming keenly aware of this on my first visit to Arizona's Canyon de Chelly, some twenty-five years ago. Canyon de Chelly is an 83,480-acre valley in northeastern Arizona, a site inhabited by the Anasazi Indians for almost a thousand years, and the location of some of their most spectacular ruins. A close friend had taken me there, not telling me where we were going or why. Getting out of the car, I walked to the cliff's edge. The 1,000-foot sheer drop gave a bird's-eye perspective of the valley: the walls of stone holding back the earth on either side, the valley's turfed floor and the sweeping channel of Chinle Wash, its bed a broad, pebbled path. The pueblos, tucked into niches of the cliffs and built of native sandstone and adobe, remain one of the most inspired examples of integrating house into landscape I have seen.

Ever since the beginning of my partnership with Wolfgang Oehme in 1971, the naturalistic gardens and landscapes we designed together have been inspired by America's rich prairie grasslands and meadows. We abandoned the clipped, tightly controlled landscaping style current in the United States up to that time. Lapping the land in sheets of grasses and bold perennials, we created a look that many have hailed as the "New American" garden. What has been less widely recognized is the role that architecture played in creating that style. Just as our planting derives from natural and native models, so too does our architecture.

William Clift, *White House at Canyon de Chelly*, 1975.

DOMESTICATING THE LANDSCAPE

You'll find architecture on any site where you choose to garden—in the topography of the land, the natural arrangement of trees, shrubs, and rocks. You can, of course, change the existing architecture. Indeed, manipulating the architecture of the site is the most powerful tool a gardener has for domesticating the landscape and for adding drama and interest.

By "domesticating" the landscape, I am referring to the process of making it comfortable and convenient for human use. That's the essence of a garden, of course, whether it's on the scale of my narrow property in Georgetown or the Canyon de Chelly. A wilderness, by contrast, may be magnificent, a superbly pleasurable aesthetic experience, but it would be inconvenient for day-to-day life. When you cut a path from your campsite to the spring or clear an area for sleeping or eating, you begin the transformation to garden.

Designing a garden, then, must begin with what we call "the program." That is, before opening the first nursery catalog, you should think long and hard about how you want the landscape to function, what you want it to do, and what it will need to accomplish those purposes. What's the best route for the path that will take you from door to street or from door to parking area? Will the herb and vegetable garden be in proximity to the kitchen? Where should you place the terrace where you plan to breakfast on pleasant weekends? Will that spot catch the warming morning sun—and be protected from the hot afternoon sun that would make the terrace unusable for the second half of the day?

SCULPTURE IN FOUR DIMENSIONS

Architecture also has an essential aesthetic role. This, of course, is what makes it most exciting, and challenging, for the average gardener. Architectural elements such as hedges, fences, and walls may be used in combination with paths to shape the experience of a visitor to the garden. In this matter, you must think of the garden not as a two-dimensional picture but rather as sculpture—a sculpture in four dimensions. That is, ideally a garden should have not only dimensions of length, width, and height but also of time. Through the use of architecture, you divide the garden into different areas and dictate the sequence in which these areas are experienced.

For example, in residential designs, I often like to attach a "secret garden" to the master bedroom. A small, peaceful space enclosed by a hedge or fence, the secret garden is normally accessible only by a door from the bedroom; the gate that provides an exit to the rest of the landscape (so that materials may be brought in and out of the garden without traveling through the house) is kept locked. This is the area of the garden in which the clients start the day, sharing an intimate breakfast when the weather is good. Or they

may end the day there, sharing a glass of wine before bed. In any case, the magic of this space is that it is experienced just at those special times.

Skillful use of architecture can also inject mystery and surprise into a landscape, by controlling and limiting the visitor's view at any given spot. I have a special affection for broad, flat landscapes. I love their expansive feel. Without the addition of an architectural frame, however, such a land-

scape has no mystery—the whole of it can be experienced in a single glance from any spot. That's a fatal defect, for it's your curiosity about what lies around the bend or behind the screen that draws you through the garden and turns a visit into a voyage of discovery.

Conversely, architecture can also be used to direct the eye. A simple but effective device is to group lawn furniture, arranging the chairs side by side, so that they look out onto a view that I want to bring to the visitor's attention. Even when the chairs are empty, the urge to check what they are aimed at is irresistible.

I also use architecture to instill drama into the landscape, to energize it and bring it to life. This is done mainly through contrast. A rectilinear area of straight lines and right angles may be boring—until you swing a curving path through it. Similarly, a ruler-straight path makes a strong statement when cutting through a landscape of relaxed, naturalistic curves.

Edges, incidentally, are a place where I find architecture especially useful. As the lines where two contrasting treatments such as lawn and flower bed or pool and deck meet, edges are inherently dramatic. I like to play to this strength by defining an edge neatly and emphatically with some frankly architectural treatment, perhaps a band of cut flagstones or a path of carefully laid brick.

MATCHMAKING

A term that our design team uses often is *marry;* we seek to marry house to garden or garden to surrounding landscape. Our design goal is to integrate these different elements so that they become inseparable parts of a single whole. Too often houses are at war with their setting because the styles of building and landscape are so dissimilar. Our goal is to make our clients' houses look as if they grew out of the site. The most effective devices we have for this are all architectural.

The easiest means of marrying house and garden is to pick up details of the house's architecture and incorporate them into the outdoor setting. An obvious example would be to use brick as a paving material in the garden around a brick house. A more sophisticated expression of the same principle would be to set a ter-

race at the foot of a back door, arranging the paving so that it continues the lines of the house itself like a floor bleeding out into the landscape.

To marry the garden to the surrounding landscape, I often use a technique perfected by the Japanese, one that they refer to as "borrowing scenery." This involves selecting a central element from a distant view and including it in the garden. In the landscape on the edge of a bay or lake, for example, I might set a pool so that it provides an echo close at hand of the more distant body of water. To enhance the effect, I might encase the pool with materials that suggest those of the beach beyond. In this way, a small detail of architecture seals the marriage of garden and surround.

ARCHITECTURE AND STYLE

Not surprisingly, the most famous examples of architecture in the garden are those that are most extreme. A striking example of an architecturally manipulated landscape is Louis XIV's breathtaking and seemingly endless expanse of barbered trees and statued promenades at Versailles (opposite). This garden has become a byword, which has produced an unfortunate side effect: with this example foremost in their minds, many gardeners assume that architecture is compatible only with a grand and formal design style (a style incompatible, in other words, with the homes of anyone other than royalty and dictators).

The reality is, however, that a strong architectural framework is especially important if your planting style is informal. A formal plan—one with a symmetrical or geometrical arrangement—provides the garden with an unmistakable, if sometimes oppressive, structure. The more spontaneous-seeming plantings of a naturalistic garden do not have that conspicuous kind of order. With them, there is a distinct danger that casual will slip into chaos, that what was intended as a garden will end up as just a vegetable mob. To prevent this the gardener must very clearly determine ahead of time how each area of the garden will be organized and how the different parts will relate. Once the broad outlines of a formal design have been established, the

planting of the garden proceeds almost automatically. An informal garden, on the other hand, involves a continual series of disjointed decisions.

It may seem contradictory, but a strong use of architecture can greatly add to a lush, sensual look in a garden. For proof of this, you need only look to what is probably the most famous English garden of the twentieth century, Sissinghurst Castle. Maintained today by the National Trust, Sissinghurst was the home of Vita Sackville-West and Harold Nicholson. Although the gardens are popularly credited to the feminine half of this partnership, in fact they represent a collaboration. Sackville-West, a famously sensitive and impetuous poet, selected the plants and decided how they would be disposed. But it was her husband, Nicholson, a self-controlled, classically inclined diplomat, who laid out the outlines of the garden, planning in detail the paths, divisions, and spaces. The impression that the resulting garden creates is all lush Sackville-West, yet she her-

self was quite frank about her debt to her husband. She explained the success of the garden as a combination of "the strictest formality of design, with the maximum informality in planting."

ORGANIZING THE GARDEN

One final way in which architecture can enhance the process of garden design is by helping the designer structure his or her thinking. For an amateur, someone with enthusiasm but little previous experience, this process can be daunting. Bombarded with instructions about "balance," "exposure," and "scale," the novice may simply freeze.

I think the best way to organize a complicated program is to reduce the garden into its basic architectural elements: the floor that is the soil, turf, herbaceous plants, or pavement; the walls of shrubbery or man-made structures that enclose the space; and the ceiling of tree canopy or arbor. Right away the would-be designer is back on familiar ground. Everyone has experience with organizing the furnishings, fixtures, and amenities within a room or suite of rooms. Draw on the principles you've learned through that, and you're ready to begin the challenging but intensely satisfying process of designing the architectural structure of your garden.

Sissinghurst Castle Garden, Kent (the National Trust), England.

ELEMENTS OF GARDEN ARCHITECTURE

chapter three

WHEN WE IMPOSE A GEOMETRIC ORDER ON THE LANDSCAPE,

WE INHABIT THE LANDSCAPE WITH HUMAN THOUGHT.

—Martha Schwartz

"THE BONES OF THE GARDEN"—THAT'S AN EXPRESSION YOU'LL HEAR gardeners use quite often. When they do, they are referring to the prominent, permanent elements that give form and structure to their landscapes. These bones may be natural—trees and rocks or perhaps a body of water—or they may be man-made. It's the man-made structural elements we are going to consider here. For important as the natural bones may be—they are what gives a site its character—the man-made ones, the paths, terraces, trellises, fences, gates, arbors, pools, and decks, are the framework with which you give a garden purpose, character, and expression. The architecture is what bounds and focuses the space. A garden may have different kinds of bones, but it's the architectural elements that are the spine.

We've already looked at the role that architecture can and must play in the garden-making process. What I want to do now is help you translate those ideas into action. To do that, it is first necessary to address the stumbling blocks that so frequently stymie less experienced gardeners. They think that to achieve a well-designed garden, they need a professional architect's experience, a pile of money and, probably, acres of land as well.

The truth is you certainly do not need a millionaire's resources; nor do you need a degree in landscape architecture. Experience is a great help, but this book will allow you to gain from mine.

Before beginning the garden-making process, you must develop a detailed, well-crafted plan. It is the one absolute prerequisite. You need to do this for two reasons. First, if you try to develop a garden off the cuff, designing with your spade as you go along, you'll never coordinate all the different parts. What's more, the resulting landscape will lack the kind of imaginative vision that is what breathes life into a garden. Second, there's a very practical reason for starting with a plan. Unlike the planting, a garden's architecture, once in place, cannot be changed without a great deal of effort and expense. The first rule of the designer on a budget is to make architectural experiments on paper, not on the ground.

Before you pick up a pencil you will have some research to do. As I noted in Chapter Two (page 21), I begin any design project by determining what is to be that particular landscape's "program of activities." The program is an outline of all the uses and activities that the garden must accommodate. I identify these by interviewing the client. In your case, of course, the process will be one of self-analysis.

What, I ask the garden's owners, do they intend to do in that space? Do they want a space for outdoor dining or entertaining? Do they like to throw big parties, or do they just have a few guests over for a quiet dinner? Maybe they like to cook and so they need a plot for vegetables and herbs. Maybe they love to fill the house with fresh flowers and will want a spot for a cutting garden. Perhaps they collect sculpture and envision the garden as an outdoor gallery. If the garden is intended as a refuge, a fountain or other water feature may be needed to mask the din from traffic or passing planes.

Investigating the clients' personal style is an essential part of establishing the program. Before I start designing, I need to know if the clients like an untamed, natural look or whether they feel more comfortable in a swept, tidy space paved and edged with stone. Do the clients prefer secluded spaces or expansive views— or both? Depending on the clients and the character of the site, the program I develop may differ drastically—

compare, for example, the program I developed for "A Fountain in New York" (page 85) with that of "A Rural Estate" (page 99).

When I've finished interviewing the client, I write out all the answers I've obtained on a sheet of paper. I keep this at hand as I work up the design. The information on that sheet not only determines the architectural features I must include, it also dictates how I divide and arrange the garden's spaces. Writing out the program is an exercise that focuses my thinking. As I review the clients' needs and dreams, I recognize all the facilities that will be needed to accommodate the life they hope to lead in the garden. At the same time, I begin to imagine how all these different facets of the garden can relate to each other. In this way, what starts as a grab bag of parts begins to assemble itself into the single, seamless whole that is a good garden.

Writing out the program also assists the design process in another, very nuts-and-bolts kind of way. I have found that reviewing the clients' answers about what they want from the garden provides useful clues about architectural details such as garden furniture and lighting systems. Such furnishings must be selected to enhance the desired activities. Similarly, the program guides my decisions about colors and textures, and paving materials—a patio that will be used for dancing parties, for instance, needs a smoother and more durable surface than one intended for occasional sunbathing.

Working out a clear, detailed program is only the beginning of the design process. Using the information gained in this manner, I apply a number of intellectual tools to develop the design itself. In a bit I'll describe the whole tool kit in detail. First, though, I want to mention five points that I believe are always key to the successful use of those tools:

Consult the House. Whenever possible, I rely on the architecture of the house to inspire my design. This relates to a process I have already referred to, of marrying the house to the land. I deal with this in detail on pages 51–65. I should mention, however, that if when I am called in to design a garden the house is being designed at the same time, I have found that success depends on good teamwork among the architect, the interior designer, and myself (for an example of this sort of partnership, see "An Island Retreat" on page 145).

Design Architectural Elements First. I always design the garden's architectural elements before deciding on the plants that will surround them. Architecture and planting must work together, eventually, as partners to bring visual unity to the garden and make the landscape work as a reflection of the owners' dreams and lifestyle. In the design process, however, the backbone comes first. Grading and sculpting the earth, and laying out terraces, steps, and walls, all contribute to the garden's seamless fit into its surroundings.

Use Care with Proportions. Endowing your spaces and the architectural elements within them with the right proportions is crucial to creating an attractive and useful garden. In part, you draw the proportion from the setting; the garden spaces should be in scale with the house, for example. A grand allée might be appropriate as the approach to a stately mansion but pretentious if fronting an intimate weekend cottage.

There's more to proportion than scale, however. The size of the outdoor spaces must be sufficient to accommodate the intended activities. A path, for example, should be wide enough to allow passage of pedestrians without crowding, and if the walk is a principal thoroughfare it's wise to make it at least 5 feet across so that two walkers can pass without jostling each other (10 feet is better in a public space). Additionally, the proportions of different areas of the garden should harmonize; if they contrast, they should do so intentionally. I borrowed the idea of a secret garden from the garden architects of the Italian Renaissance. They used to tuck a small, enclosed space of this sort into some corner of their princely landscapes to provide a retreat for more personal moments. The magic of this *giardino segreto* lies in the compact proportions, which seem marvelously intimate by comparison to the grand parterres and avenues all around.

Getting the proportions right is still a challenge for me after many years of experience. How do you learn proportion? By looking around, by reading, by trusting your own eyes.

Choose Materials Carefully. In large part, I rely on the materials to pull a garden together. One secret to making this work is choosing the materials to suit the place. I take cues from the landscape that surrounds the house and from the architectural character of the building, and I select the best construction materials the budget will allow (see the Simmons and Diamond gardens on pages 123 and 171).

In general, I select materials that are indigenous to the region and treat them according to local tradition. This is important because often what works in one region doesn't sit well elsewhere. For instance, I've found that limestone, which is quarried locally in the Middle West, looks very much at home in the gardens of that region. Pennsylvania bluestone belongs to the mid-Atlantic region. The objections may be practical as well as aesthetic. Terra-cotta tile, for instance, looks very much at home in the warm, sunny Florida landscape and is also quite durable in an outdoor setting there. The same material not only looks out of place in a cloudy northern garden but also soon disintegrates under the stress of the North's seasonal freezing and thawing.

To select materials that are suited to your climate and your design, consult with local suppliers and visit local gardens to see what is traditionally used in your area. To best enhance your design, the materials should exude quality, warmth, and strength. Whenever possible, they should also reflect those of the house — which leads to the following point.

Know When to Stop.   A common, though ineffective, trick for hiding the defects of a poor landscape design is to mask them with plantings or furnishings. What few gardeners realize is that it's just as easy to obscure a good design in this fashion.

We've all heard the stock advice: hide the unattractive view with a screen of fencing or evergreens; bury that old stump under a swathe of greenery. Of course, such expedients can work, but you must take care to integrate the screen or mask into the greater design. Otherwise, your obtrusive fix may only draw attention to the problem.

What's worse, though, is when I see a similar kind of treatment inadvertently applied to good bones. It's like draping doilies all over a fine piece of furniture. If you've taken the time to analyze the site and your needs, and then developed an attractive architectural framework that addresses both, you should let this speak out. Resist the urge to fill every available space with plantings or furnishings. Remember that empty space can be an eloquent statement in its own right. Empty space is an essential counterpoint to the mass of the built elements. It's the setting that shows off the plantings. The best rule is that before installing any new element in the garden, ask yourself whether it is essential and how it will contribute to the effect of your design.

To return to the design tools: This is a term that I apply not only to the actual instruments with which I sketch but also to a variety of precepts that guide the imaginative part of the design. Some of them may seem counterintuitive, if not downright wrong; these you will have to take on faith.

Explore. Look around, photograph, sketch, and research the real world of other people's gardens. What you see will become the vocabulary you use in creating or refining your own garden. When I travel I investigate how gardens are designed and used in other cultures. When at home I continue to explore the world's gardens through books.

Ask Questions. In snooping around I ask myself, what is so different about that garden? Why do I prefer this stonework or that pond? By looking carefully, I begin to discern the important differences among gardens. I note the siting of each garden, the line of a hedge or placement of a water feature, the exploitation of existing shade from large trees. I look for use of a material—brick or stone or wood inspired or "pulled out" (see page 145) from the materials of the house itself. Above all, if I like a garden, I try to analyze what it is that makes this a landscape I would like to inhabit.

Draw Your Dream. Use graph paper to sketch the approximate proportions of your home. Situate the house in the context of its landscape—whether it's a rural tract, suburban neighborhood, or urban backyard. Then draw the garden of your dreams. Make many drawings, and pursue your ideas wherever they take you. The result may be ridiculous, but it may also be sublime. If you can imagine it, draw it. Then scale the finished drawing to your needs and budget.

Think Big. This is the most important and least self-evident principle underlying a wonderful garden. Always err on the side of too big. It took a long time for me to understand this.

Designing too small is the most common blunder among professional and lay gardeners alike, and it is always a mistake. The reason for this is that there are few fixed boundaries out of doors to contain your line of sight or movement. In such an expansive setting, small typically looks skimpy; generous sizing works.

This rule applies to the proportion that you give to the spaces you create and to individual architectural features as well. You should, for example, design larger terraces and water features than you think the site can afford. A little experiment will prove the wisdom of this. Measure the length and width of a chaise longue, and double or even quadruple that space. Will the terrace you are contemplating accommodate this fairly standard use?

Be generous too in the width and length you allow for walkways and retaining walls. The proportion of these utilitarian features must reflect their function in the site—a walk has to reach from beginning point to goal, and a retaining wall must be high enough to contain the slope. However, don't restrict such features to the minimum dimensions necessary. They also play an important aesthetic role in tying the house to the landscape and should be given a proper mass.

Surprisingly, the rule of bigger being better applies especially to small gardens. Nothing makes a small space look smaller than skimpy built elements. A cramped terrace, a path that's too narrow, or a bathtub-sized pond will only create visual discomfort by reminding you of your garden's tiny space. Even the smallest areas should contain generously sized elements—they may simply contain fewer of them.

Build a Model. Create a three-dimensional view of the garden you would like to have, using balsa wood, cardboard, foam core, clay, and cork. You can find these materials at your local craft store. Even if you have never built a model, these materials are flexible and easy to work with. Don't be afraid to play with them and to make several attempts. This process helps you clarify what it is you really want, rather than just whatever it is you think your space and budget will allow. A model also provides one of the best tools for

studying the effect of different proportions.

Rehearse. Do this before you dig. Lay out paths and pond sizes with string or garden hose to see the actual scale of what you're building. Bring furniture out into the garden and arrange it where you intend to create eating or sitting spots. This will help you establish if your proposed design allows sufficient space to permit easy navigation *around* chairs and tables (let alone those chaise longues) on a prospective terrace or deck. Consider the amount of room you would need if you wanted to have dancing on the terrace—and take a turn around the space. This is a *rehearsal,* and it's an essential step before you get out the shovels and requisition quantities of brick and stone. After all, you may discover that if you don't expand that terrace, you'll be stepping on your partner's toe.

Choose Bold Architectural Elements. Don't hold back when selecting elements such as gates, walls, arbors, containers, and fountains, and experiment with using color and strong sculptural forms. Stick your neck out—dramatic lighting or an oversized object can make your garden unique. Designing a garden should be fun. It's an opportunity to make a statement, so feel free to express yourself strongly.

Create Outdoor "Rooms." Dividing the garden into a series of discrete spaces or "rooms" is a classic way to organize the landscape. This type of design has tremendous flexibility, making it possible to pursue a multitude of different experiences and activities in a relatively small area. One room, for example, might function as an elegant outdoor dining space; the diners need not even be aware of the utilitarian kitchen garden on the other side of a hedge or fence. A clever use of rooms is also one of the most effective devices for adding mystery to a garden (see below).

There are other means for delineating the spaces that are subtler than physical barriers yet effective nevertheless. I often use "carpets" of pavement to define different spaces. A dining area and the adjacent cooking area, for example, might both be paved, but the stone or brick laid in two different patterns so that a distinction is made. You may not consciously notice the change, at least at first, but you will be aware of it at some level and feel a sense of transition as you move from one area to the other. If handled skillfully, such paving patterns fulfill the same function as do your home's interior walls in dividing and ordering the space.

Create Mystery. Visual stops and barriers are equally important in enhancing the experience of the garden. Use sculpture, containers, arbors, and lattices—as well as plantings—to divide the space. By creating layers of experience, these tangible and intangible screens deepen the garden's effect, even if the total space is actually small. Such screens also endow the garden with an exciting sense of mystery: you can't help wondering what is beyond that wall, trellis, hedge, or fence and what you'd find at the end of that path disappearing around the corner. Don't neglect the auditory element. The sound of running water or of wind rustling through grasses also catches and holds our interest, thus creating another layer of experience through which to pass as you progress through the garden.

Use Lighting as a Tool. Artificial lighting manipulates light and shadow out of doors, just as it does inside your home. It can be a powerful year-round tool in the garden—even the winter garden can be lit at night to tailor the view from and of your home. Installing lights also domesticates the outdoor space, further blurring the distinction between indoors and out.

Treat Small Spaces Geometrically. A small outdoor space naturally has the feeling of a room and as such relates more closely to the interior of the house. Indeed, the most effective way of handling such spaces is, as a rule, to treat them as outdoor extensions of the house. Give them a strong, geometrical archi-tecture, one that pulls out the architecture of the indoor rooms.

Treat Large Spaces with Curves.   If your garden is large, draw pools, paths, and fences in broad, relaxed strokes to suit the topography. Sweeping lines have an exciting energy, and help to carry the eye through the length of the garden by pulling it from the house to the distant views. On an expansive site, recti-linear walls and paths stretched away from the house look and feel stingy.

Set an Example.   Not only should the design of your garden seem of a piece with your home, it should also fit the context of the architecture in your neighborhood—to a point. Use materials that don't clash with the vernacular, but don't hold yourself back if your surroundings are not up to your standards. Don't be afraid to raise the level of design in your neighborhood—be adventurous.

Follow Your Local Building Code.   Every jurisdiction has its own building code, which must be followed when designing your garden. The code itself will often provide detailed regulations for the design of elements such as walls, pools, and fences. Permits are required, and inspections by the permit officer must be scheduled at various stages of construction. If your garden is in a historic district it may be necessary to secure approval by an appropriate authority before a permit for construction will be issued. Follow the laws carefully, and use licensed contractors as required for approvals.

These tools are meant to serve you in the design process as they serve me. I'll add to it an indispensable bit of wisdom from the great modern landscape architect Thomas Church: "The place to start with is yourself." That in fact should top your list of design tools.

Learning how to apply these tools to best effect is mostly a matter of experience. I'll give you a head start on that and provide a series of object lessons. In the following pages I share my own design experience by guiding you through twelve gardens that I've created. I selected them to demonstrate the fundamental role architecture plays in the construction of dramatic gardens. The gardens are presented either in the form

of detailed case studies, which describe the process of designing and building the entire project, or as cameos, which include brief textual and visual snapshots of a particularly relevant aspect of that garden. Introductory text precedes each "garden tour"; it highlights the central idea that the case study illustrates in detail. For example, Chapter 5 first describes how to incorporate art in the garden and is then followed by three cameos of superb gardens that incorporate mosaics and sculpture as part of their architecture.

These extraordinary landscapes all have what I regard as particularly good bone structure. They embody the design principles, materials, and textures that create the foundation for a magnificent year-round garden. Like good bone structure in a human face, good bone structure in the garden retains its grace and beauty even after the bloom fades.

Each of the following case studies reveals how all the pieces of the garden's architecture come together to create a pleasing whole. Although many of these gardens benefited from generous budgets, each contains effects and features that are easy to achieve at a more modest cost. By exploring these gardens in detail, you'll learn how to identify and "read" their exceptional features and how to use the elements responsible for their ineffable magic. Then you can move to the next level: that of planning and building the architecture of your own garden.

So let's begin.

PART TWO

GARDEN STUDIES

PULLING THE ARCHITECTURE OF
THE HOUSE INTO THE GARDEN

chapter four

OUR HOUSE IS OUR CORNER OF THE WORLD....IT IS OUR FIRST

UNIVERSE, A REAL COSMOS IN EVERY SENSE OF THE WORD.

—*Gaston Bachelard*

A

S I PULLED UP TO OPRAH WINFREY'S FRONT DOOR FOR THE FIRST TIME,

my immediate impression was that her house was divorced from its setting. Built in an elegant French chateau

style, the house was visibly uncomfortable with the matter-of-fact midwestern farmland that surrounded it.

Nothing had been done to ease the transition from one to the other—the house and site weren't talking.

I felt that some sort of détente was the first priority, and I began to explain the need for a cross-cultural

marriage to Oprah. She understood immediately, seizing on the idea with her famous energy and enthusiasm.

Over the next four years, we worked together to create an architectural context around the house, including

newly installed terraces and walls. The materials we selected, brick framed with limestone, echoed the house,

yet this architecture also conformed to the surrounding countryside, adopting its long, horizontal lines. In this

way we quite literally pulled the house out into the site.

You must keep this relationship in mind as you design. Most of us, when we set out to make a garden, create it around our home. In doing so, we must deal with natural elements such as topography, climate, and soil. Good gardeners consult the site and strive to work with, rather than against, nature. However, a residential landscape, a home garden, is always a marriage, and you must make sure that not only the site but also the other man-made partner, the house, is accommodated. The style and form of the garden must flow from house as well as land.

Usually when I undertake a residential project, I encounter one of three situations. The house may be spectacular. In that case, I treat it like an exquisite diamond whose beauty should be enhanced and set off by a subtle and unassuming setting. At the other extreme, I sometimes find that the house suffers from such obvious aesthetic flaws that it is going to detract visually from whatever sort of garden I may create around it. The role of the landscaping then becomes to tactfully mask the house, to hide its faults. More often than not, though, the situation I encounter lies between these two extremes. Both house and site have their strengths, both have their interest, but because they aren't working toward the same end they each diminish the impact of the other. When the dissonance of house and garden causes them both to be less than what they should be, then my task is simply that of architectural marriage counselor.

Sometimes clients will call me in to design the landscape for a house that is itself still in the process of being designed. In such cases, I can work with the architect of the house, and the marriage of house and garden may become a process of give and take. More often, however, my commission is to design a garden around an existing house. When that is so, I begin by listening to the house.

Generally, after spending a few minutes in the clients' house and neighborhood, I can already tell a great deal about their interests and needs and consequently about the kind of garden they will find enjoyable and useful. Immediately upon arriving, a brief survey of the surrounding houses and a quick look at the character of their landscapes suggest to me the kind of environment that my clients find congenial. I follow this by examining the clients' house and property to see how they fit into the larger landscape. As I walk up to the front door, I note opportunities—an outstanding or unusual tree, perhaps—and obvious problems such as excessive street noises. By the time I'm inside talking to my clients, even if I am meeting them for the first time, I can make some educated suggestions about directions to take their garden.

Meanwhile, I am sizing up the interior of the house. It provides clues about the clients' taste and also about how they are likely to relate to their garden. If the house is neat and in good repair, I'm reassured that they'll make time for the garden too and tend it well. If the draperies are shabby, the colors muddy, and the house in general disrepair, my hunch is that the garden won't get enough of their attention either. Is this just my house-proud Dutch ancestors speaking through me? I don't think so, for I have often found that these first impressions are borne out by subsequent experience with the clients. Though not in all cases — good gardeners are not always good housekeepers.

To build on these initial observations, I spend a bit of time studying the house so that I thoroughly understand its plan, construction, and style. This lets me begin to imagine how I can "pull" its spaces and materials out into the landscape. This is accomplished mainly through the architecture I design for the garden.

My goal is to continue the themes and style of the house out into the garden and thereby integrate the two. I might surround a stately and substantial Victorian home with a verandah to create a place of transition between indoors and out. I might echo the woodwork of the house's interior with heavy handrails and balustrades. Recently I designed the setting for a magnificent Japanese-inspired house in the Low Country of coastal South Carolina (page 145). To escape the floods that periodically wash over this site, the house was set on pilings. To marry this house to its site, I surrounded it with a cascade of wooden decks.

In the case study that I have chosen to illustrate this marriage process, the house was an English-flavored stone cottage (page 51). You'll see how I extended it into the garden via stone walls that were crafted to match the masonry of the house and then reinforced this sense of connection by accenting the garden with rustic, cottage-style details such as sturdy wooden gates, fences, and lattices.

Pulling out the architecture, however, is more than just a matter of echoing style. It also requires making a careful inventory of the house's rooms and their uses. The results of this then influence the arrangement of the outdoor spaces. Convenience, for instance, usually dictates that an outdoor dining space should adjoin the kitchen. Linking those two areas also creates a smoother interface between indoor and outdoor life. Often, though, the connection is more subtle. One effective device is to extend the proportions of the rooms into the outdoors, just as the Japanese traditionally use the dimensions of a tatami mat both inside and outside (page 7). That South Carolina house I described above was laid out on an 8-foot grid. That is, the dimensions of each interior space were some multiple of the basic 8-foot unit. I adopted the same grid for the rectangular blocks of planks with which I surfaced the deck. As a result, decks and house don't feel like adjoining spaces; they feel like different parts of a whole.

As I noted earlier, the strengths or limitations of the house's architecture also shape my treatment of the landscape and so the terms of the marriage.

You might be so lucky as to own an architectural gem, such as the nineteenth-century rural estate detailed in Chapter 6 (page 99). The house in that case was a lovingly constructed classic. There was no ugly foundation to hide, so there was no need to screen the base with shrubbery. Instead, I set the house like a jewel, surrounding it with a simple but elegant lawn that wouldn't obscure its beautiful lines. As this example indicates, there's far less need for architectural transitions such as decks, arbors, and walls when the house's designer has already suited the structure to the site and worked out all its details so fully and so well.

What, however, do you do if your house is plain or downright unattractive? In that case, you can use the garden to give it what amounts to a face-lift. A skillful arrangement of architectural elements such as trellises, lattice work, pergolas, flights of stairs, low walls, and terraces can not only hide a house's flaws, they can add drama and energize an otherwise ordinary house. Vines can soften edges and lines that are ugly or abrupt. Interrupting a large expanse of masonry with a relief of soft-textured greenery—the silhouette of a tree or shrub—can greatly relieve the impression of heaviness.

A skillful application of paint can also work a striking change in the impression that a house makes. A neutral earth tone such as a beige will make a house seem to recede into the landscape. Painting the walls and details—window frames, doors, trim, and so on—in related hues can often pull together all the parts of a less than stellar house. You can, in short, play up or play down the various features of a house.

One aspect of this marrying process is that the architecture you create outside will have a strong effect on what you experience of its interior. Your first encounter with the house is the view from outside; when you see the house in its landscape setting, and after you have gone in, the views from the window are all of the garden. Either way, the landscape has tremendous influence on setting the mood. In addition, though, I find that changes to the garden architecture have another, subtler transformative effect. Commonly, the changes I make to the outdoor materials begin to influence the clients' choices of indoor materials: the architecture that I have pulled out begins to be pulled back in.

A NEW WORLD COTTAGE

GARDEN AND HOUSE BELONG TOGETHER,
VISUALLY AND ACTUALLY.

—*Thomas Church*

THERE ARE MARRIAGES MADE IN HEAVEN, AND THEN THERE ARE MARRIAGES created on the drafting table. The following story is about a marriage of the latter type, a wedding of house and land that was and is one of the happiest and most harmonious I have ever achieved.

The opportunity sprang from a common situation. The children had grown, and the couple who owned the house suddenly found it half empty but full of potential. After decades of child rearing, the owners of the house had the chance to select a new pattern of life—the possibilities seemed endless. Often people find this sort of drastic change disorienting and traumatic. They change partners or move out of town in a self-conscious, often desperate, stab at renewal. This couple, however, responded in a less dramatic but far more positive and, ultimately, more transformative way. They chose to remain in their old setting but wished to re-create it. With my help, they worked out a new relationship between their shelter and the landscape around it. In the process, they also explored and redefined patterns of their own life.

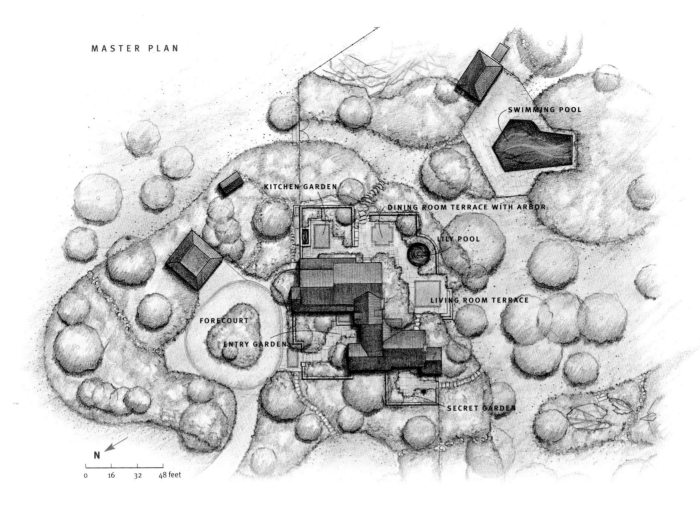

The clients in this case came to me for help because they had admired an enclosed secret garden that I designed for one of their friends. As part of their new lifestyle, they imagined attaching a garden of this same sort to their own master bedroom. As soon as I saw the site, I knew they could do much more.

The 1920s vintage stone and shingle cottage was situated on 9 acres in a semirural neighborhood to the north of New York City; the clients had been using it as a weekend retreat but now intended to spend more time there. They had just enhanced its handcrafted charm with an architectural renovation, which had given the house the air of an English Cotswold cottage.

The site was marked with rugged, moody outcroppings of granite and sheltered by lofty, venerable red oaks and sugar maples. Because nearly every one of the house's rooms communicated directly with the outdoors, I saw an unusual potential for interaction between house and landscape.

The landscaping immediately around the house consisted of little more than a brick terrace and a few garden beds. Although they did not detract from the site's latent charm, these additions did little to enhance it. The trees, which should have been a tremendous asset, also failed to contribute much to the garden. The existing landscaping, such as it was, made no use of them. Their only effect on the area around the house was to make it dark and somber. Overall, as I looked at the

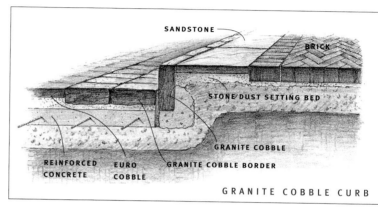

GRANITE COBBLE CURB

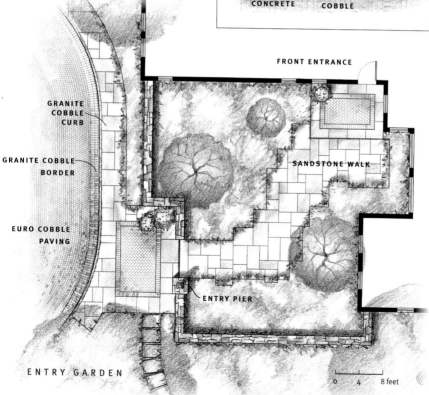

ENTRY GARDEN

0   4   8 feet

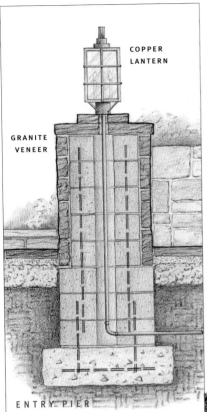

COPPER
LANTERN

GRANITE
VENEER

ENTRY PIER

landscaping, I found it lacking in the sense of drama that the site clearly deserved. Rather than benefiting from the site's natural beauty, the house and garden were overshadowed by it.

My clients' love of England and the way that expressed itself in the house's architecture made my choice of a style for the garden easy. I decided to present them with a New World interpretation of the cottage gardens they had enjoyed during trips across the Atlantic. This would establish one link between house and garden, and I decided to add another: building on the client's desire for a secret garden, I saw that developing the area immediately surrounding the house as a series of garden rooms would allow me to capitalize on the neglected opportunity mentioned above, the many points of access from house to landscape.

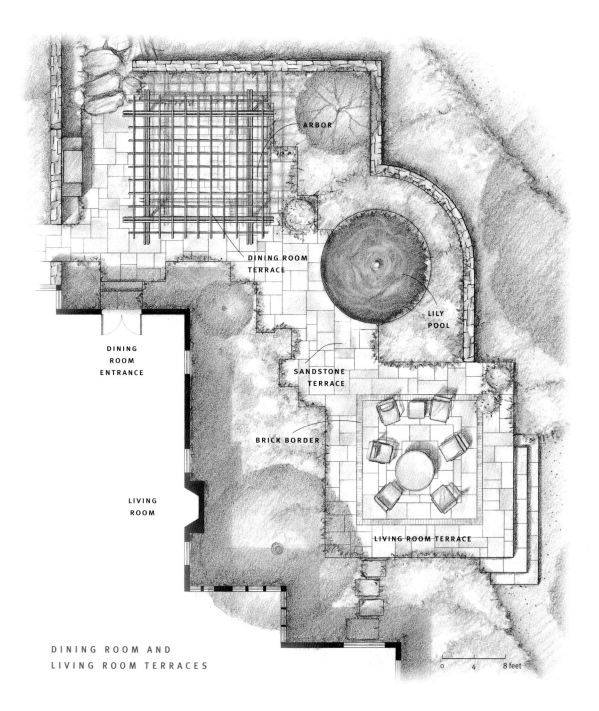

ARBOR

DINING ROOM
TERRACE

DINING
ROOM
ENTRANCE

LILY
POOL

SANDSTONE
TERRACE

BRICK BORDER

LIVING
ROOM

LIVING ROOM TERRACE

DINING ROOM AND
LIVING ROOM TERRACES

0   4   8 feet

By associating indoor spaces with outdoor spaces of a related purpose and architec-

tural style, I could practically erase the distinction between house and garden, turning

the two parts into a single whole.

Stone, enduring and even improving with age, was the material of choice for

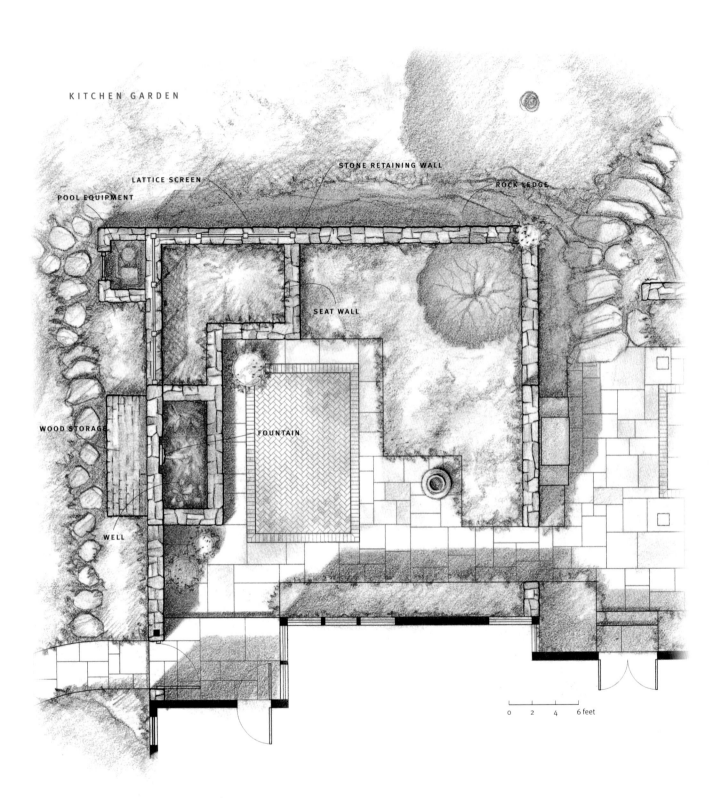

KITCHEN GARDEN

STONE RETAINING WALL

LATTICE SCREEN

ROCK LEDGE

POOL EQUIPMENT

SEAT WALL

WOOD STORAGE

FOUNTAIN

WELL

0   2   4   6 feet

the Old World builders. Fortunately, the clients' budget allowed me to use it here. I used it first in creating a new approach to the house. I relocated the driveway, replacing an unimaginative, straight-ahead orientation with a grand, sweeping curve. Where it drew near to the house, I gave the drive and forecourt a cobbled surface, finishing it around the edge with a double band of Belgian granite blocks. Then, with the same stone that had been used to build the foundation and walls of the house, I created a series of neatly finished walls to organize the garden. Low 16-inch-thick walls frame the entry garden by the front door; another low wall surrounds the kitchen garden. Similar walls frame all the outdoor garden rooms too, though the one enclosing the secret garden is taller for privacy and mystery.

The patterning of the paving was the device I used to define the garden rooms. A smooth and stately floor of cut sandstone surfaces the paths and terraces surrounding the house. Into this, I embedded carefully placed patterns of brick. A mat of brick marks the pavement right outside the front door; larger brick carpets identify the various rooms, and the contrast between the patterns in which the bricks are laid creates a sense of transition as you move from one garden room to another. This too

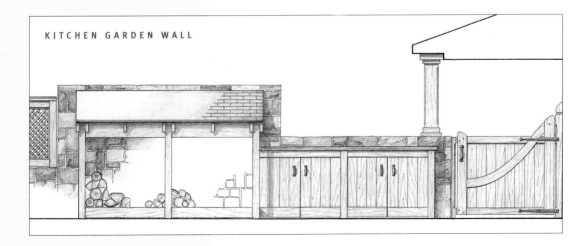

KITCHEN GARDEN WALL

was related to the house: the dimensions and scale of the carpets are related to those of the adjoining rooms inside the house.

The kitchen garden can be entered directly from the kitchen or through a cedar gate from a path that flanks the house. The bricks in this terrace are laid in a herringbone pattern. A low ledge invites you to sit beside the well and contemplate the fountain—a mask of Boreas, the spirit of the north wind, a handsome architectural fragment salvaged from a demolished building. The well is a handy place to rest or dip out a bucket of water for the cutting garden of herbs and flowers. During at least three seasons of the year, this is the favorite gathering place for morning coffee. By extending the roofline from the clients' new kitchen addition out to the garden wall, we created a covered porch that shelters the cook when he or she ventures out for a sprig of herbs during rainy weather.

The kitchen garden opens on the dining room terrace, whose carpet was formed by enclosing rectangles of the sandstone with an austere band of brick. To shelter this space from the summer sun and enhance the sense of enclosure, this area is shaded by an intricate 14-by-14-foot cypress arbor. Silver lace vine and wisteria cover this during the growing season. In winter you can see more clearly the

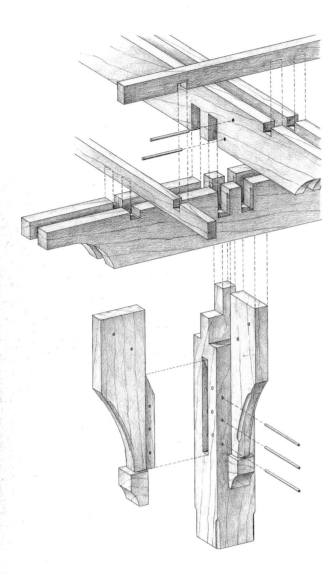

DINING TERRACE ARBOR
WITH ALL WOOD JOINERY

fine detailing of the construction—the timbers have been carefully fitted together, joined without the use of nails or metal fasteners.

Around the corner from the dining room terrace you'll find a circular lily pool and, farther on, the living room terrace, which also serves the master bedroom. As elsewhere, stone walls define each of these garden rooms, and each relates to the adjoining room in the house. Descend from this terrace, move a few steps onto the lawn—and the stone path disappears.

Around another bend, though, along an approach unmarked by any path, you come up against a high stone wall. Pass through its gate, and you discover the longed-for secret garden, seat of solitude and repose (see page 55).

Although the other garden rooms are open for access on several sides, this room reveals its secrets reluctantly. It has two doorways: the gate in the stone wall and the doors leading to the bedroom and study. Here the defining wall is high enough for seclusion, but it does not shut out light. The garden's dimensions—

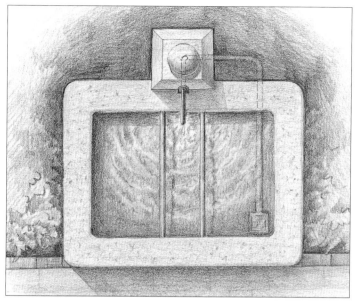

20 by 30 feet—are generous
but not oversized.

The furnishings of this
hideaway are few but fine.
A rectangular granite cistern
with a handmade bronze
spout stands at one end. Two
brass bars are notched into
the granite trough where you
can fill a pail to water the
garden. A marble medallion
depicting the American eagle
adorns the stone wall, and a
massive terra-cotta urn from

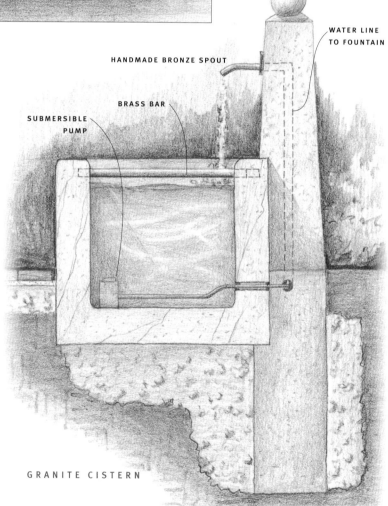

WATER LINE
TO FOUNTAIN

HANDMADE BRONZE SPOUT

BRASS BAR

SUBMERSIBLE
PUMP

GRANITE CISTERN

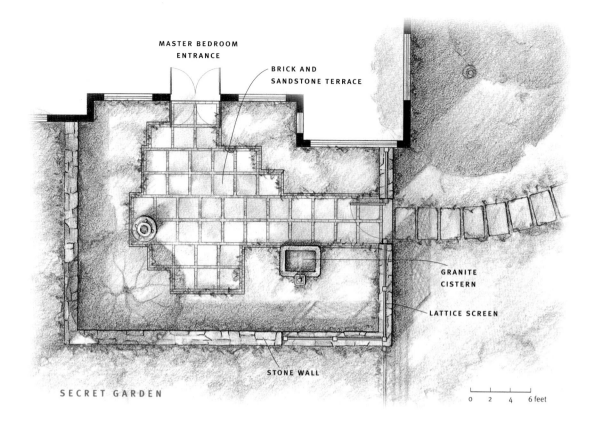

MASTER BEDROOM
ENTRANCE

BRICK AND
SANDSTONE TERRACE

GRANITE
CISTERN

LATTICE SCREEN

STONE WALL

SECRET GARDEN

0   2   4   6 feet

Greece stands at one end. The pavement of this room is constructed of sandstone squares with

intervening brick ribs, or "stringers," dividing the whole into an irregular pattern of squares. Patches

of deep green moss have grown up here and there on the stones. Containers that brim with flowers

in summer are capped with moss in winter.

The countrified note struck by this cottage's complex of outdoor rooms lends a more parklike

air to the neatly clipped sward that surrounds it. By echoing with its outcrops and columnar trunks the

vistas of surrounding woods and hills, the "park" helps to integrate the garden into the larger land-

scape.

Surprisingly, perhaps, the complex of garden walls also contributes to the increased sense

of space. Because the garden isn't all visible from any one point, there's no apparent limit to its

size. Moreover, as you walk through it, there is always a sense of mystery and expectation to draw you on. Every time you turn a corner or pass through a gap in a wall, you find yet another beautifully textured garden space. Views that are hidden in one place are abruptly revealed in another. In each space the arrangement of water, plants, and materials is just different enough from that of the other rooms to give this one the sense of a new adventure to be experienced and enjoyed.

Throughout, the reference continues to be the house. Even the scale and proportions of the large double-cedar gates (installed to keep out deer) mirror those found in the house. The sturdiness and grace of all the architectural proportions, from the depth of the walls to the circumference

of the pond and the height of the gateposts, intimately connect the original cottage with its Cotswold-inspired, but profoundly American, garden. As a essay in redefining the life of two empty-nesting adults, it has also had a surprising sort of success: the attraction of this new setting has helped draw back in the family, making the intended retreat a favorite gathering place for visiting children and grandchildren.

ART BELONGS IN THE GARDEN

chapter five

I HAVE FOUND IT HELPFUL TO THINK OF A GARDEN AS SCULPTURE. NOT
SCULPTURE IN THE ORDINARY SENSE OF AN OBJECT TO BE VIEWED. BUT
SCULPTURE THAT IS LARGE ENOUGH AND PERFORATED ENOUGH TO WALK
THROUGH. AND OPEN ENOUGH TO PRESENT NO BARRIER TO MOVEMENT, AND
BROKEN ENOUGH TO GUIDE THE EXPERIENCE WHICH IS ESSENTIALLY A COM-
MUNION WITH THE SKY.

—James C. Rose

AS STRONGLY AS I FEEL ABOUT THE POWER AND VALUE OF ART, I DO NOT AGREE

with those who treat it as something ethereal, something to be venerated in seclusion. On the contrary, I

believe that the processes both of making and enjoying art should be a part of all our daily lives. This means

that precious as the finished product may be, I don't like to see it treated as untouchable—pinned like a but-

terfly behind a pane of glass. Art should inhabit the places we inhabit. Above all (given my predilections), I

want to see it in the garden.

Taking art off its pedestal and turning it loose in the landscape has been one of my passions over the

years. In my work, plants, architecture, and sculpture each contribute to the dynamic nature of a garden and

influence its changing silhouette.

A garden, as I see it, is a work of art. When I design, I use all the elements at hand—light, temperature, water, stone, steel, and organic and geological forms—to create a finished, integrated space. This makes the garden a natural setting for art. Like the other elements of the garden, the art must be fully integrated into the design. When I am successful at this, the result is a landscape in which it's impossible to distinguish where the functional elements of the design end and where the aesthetic elements begin. Art, architecture, and plantings should combine so completely that it's hard to imagine any one of them existing without the others. Thus, art mingles with daily life—for my gardens are places made to be lived in.

This goal of integration is my motivation for defiance of a conventional practice. I don't like to raise garden art aloft, setting it up on an elevated base, superior and aloof. Instead, I prefer to bring it down to earth. When sculpture literally steps off its plinth to wander among grasses, seedpods, and sunbeams, the garden comes alive. Wit and ideas mingle with the effects of light and wind as the landscape becomes a "movable feast" for the mind and senses.

A further effect of this treatment, one that especially fascinates me, is the new dimension that integration with a garden lends to the artworks. Any experienced gardener knows the power that the change of seasons has to transform their plants; once art merges with the garden, it too undergoes seasonal metamorphoses. Thus, art can appear clothed or unclothed, depending on the season. In my own garden, for example, the spheres by sculptor Grace Knowlton are almost entirely hidden in summertime by the thick foliage of a bold ornamental grass, *Miscanthus giganteus*. The spheres just peek out from behind the fronds, hinting at something wonderful but unseen. In winter, though, the egglike, earthy forms shed their leafy cover and stand exposed. Their curves set off in dramatic fashion the stark vertical profiles of

THE MINTZ GARDEN

A FEW YEARS AGO AN OLD NEIGHBORHOOD BANK BUILDING IN WASHINGTON, D.C., presented me with a second chance. A stately block of limestone that filled a corner lot among the magnificent houses of East Capitol Street, the bank had the dignified presence of a bespectacled old gentleman. When I first saw it, though, it was about to undergo a transformation. A local physician, Dr. Gary Mintz, had purchased it and was renovating it as his private home. He commissioned me to design what would be a small, but highly visible, garden.

The job intrigued me for two reasons. First, this bank had been the sister branch to another, virtually identical bank just a few blocks away. My partner and I had bought that building more than twenty years earlier to house the offices of Oehme, van Sweden & Associates. I had designed the landscape surrounding our building. Now I was being given the opportunity to address the same context for a matching site and structure. But this time, I was designing for residential use.

There was a second reason that this commission excited me. My new client had a remarkable collection of modern art, and he wanted to incorporate some of his sculpture into the garden. This was both a challenge and an opportunity, and it would certainly shape the architecture I evolved for his site.

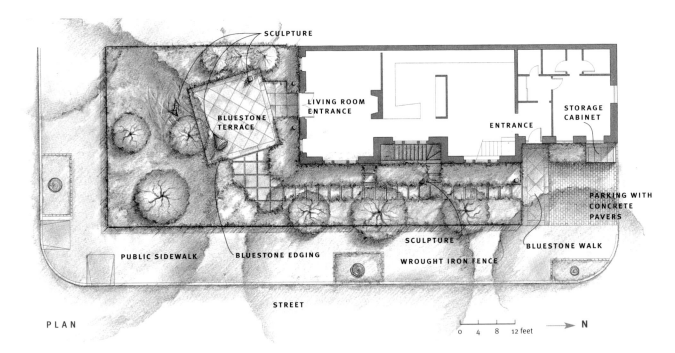

SCULPTURE

LIVING ROOM
ENTRANCE

BLUESTONE
TERRACE

STORAGE
CABINET

ENTRANCE

PARKING WITH
CONCRETE
PAVERS

PUBLIC SIDEWALK

BLUESTONE EDGING

SCULPTURE

BLUESTONE WALK

WROUGHT IRON FENCE

STREET

PLAN

0   4   8   12 feet   N

Not only did I have to accommodate the art, but because this was a home, not just a gallery, I also had to allow for a range of other uses in the same space. And space was tight: the garden had only the leftover part of a 30-by-100-foot city lot to occupy. What's more, the garden was to lie on the street side of the building. The client wanted privacy yet wanted to share his garden with passersby, even at night, when the garden must be subtly (not glaringly) illuminated.

As a commercial building, the bank had been built to expedite traffic in and out with a pair of monumental front doors on East Capitol Street. The scale of these doors was inappropriate for a private residence, and a new entrance had been created on the building's adjoining side. The old doors remained, though, and would certainly confuse visitors unless I deemphasized the former entrance and redirected traffic. In addition, I wanted to create a less direct approach to the house, to discreetly veil what was going on in the garden. However, I certainly didn't want to obscure this building's handsome architecture.

The doctor also had a number of practical requirements. He wanted a shelter in which to conceal trash cans and store tools, and a place to park a small car. He also wanted a patio of a size adequate for outdoor entertaining. Fitting all of these elements together in such a small space while still accommodating the aesthetic goals was like putting together the pieces of a Chinese puzzle.

To keep the architecture of the garden from obtruding, I chose materials that harmonized with those of the surrounding neighborhood. I used an elegant but understated bluestone for paving and paths. I selected black-enameled steel pickets topped with sculptural spherical finials for the fencing to mark the garden's perimeter. I reinforced this act of enclosure by backing the fence with drifts of tall grasses, peren-

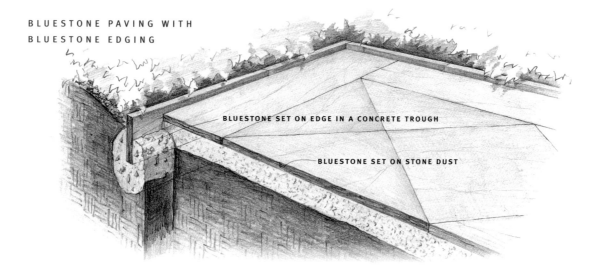

BLUESTONE PAVING WITH
BLUESTONE EDGING

BLUESTONE SET ON EDGE IN A CONCRETE TROUGH

BLUESTONE SET ON STONE DUST

nials, shrubs, and compact trees, including several Foster hollies. This visual filter satisfied another of the doctor's desires. Dr. Mintz wanted privacy but didn't want the garden to block the views from the street, or out of the house, entirely.

The garden's organization, however—that is, the arrangement of the elements within it—I drew from the building's interior. In redesigning this, the renovating architect had created a number of off-axis elements that didn't follow the bank's

original front-to-back, side-to-side layout. Taking my cue from this, when I set a bluestone patio outside the original bank doors, I twisted it off center, laying the stones on a diagonal to the central axis of the building. This little twist kept the patio's placement from seeming obvious and added a bit of energy and dramatic tension to the garden.

The building's neoclassical architecture dictated a classic treatment of materials in the garden. All the edges where pavers meet are neat and bordered with similar stone. I set a file of bluestone flags from the new front entrance around to the patio. The new front walk I gave a more elaborate treatment, to enhance its air of importance. This I made a runner of meticulously cut bluestone set in a diamond pattern, like the floors I had admired in paintings by the Flemish masters.

The parking area is paved with concrete cobbles. We constructed a simple tongue-and-groove wooden storage shed with a copper standing-seam roof to hide the trash receptacles and then framed this with three *Mahonia aquifolium*.

The real story in this garden, though, is the art. Dr. Mintz's collection of contemporary sculpture called for a beautiful, understated backdrop. Each piece is dis-

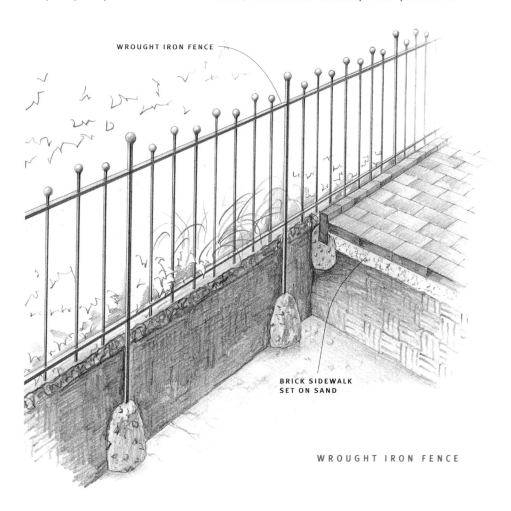

WROUGHT IRON FENCE

BRICK SIDEWALK
SET ON SAND

WROUGHT IRON FENCE

played against a lacy, semitransparent screen of tree limbs and grasses. One comes upon each work of art suddenly; each piece has the feel of being a "found" object—as if one had wandered onto an urban archaeological site full of unexpected riches.

Three sculptures focus the front garden. A kinetic stainless steel sculpture by George Rickey moves with the breeze, the two windmilling L-shaped arms catching the sun, never quite meeting (see page 76). An enormous ceramic cone by Paul Chaleff, brown and green with copper overtones, rests impressively on the front terrace (see page 76). In the opposite corner of the terrace stands an elegant, columnar 3-foot sculpture by Lee Hervey, *Time Totem,* a construction of slate, sandstone, and sandblasted glass. You see these sculptures in the front garden, peeking through veils of perennials—mostly alliums. The surrounding trees are up to their limbs, seemingly drowning in grasses, even in midwinter.

A fourth sculpture (pictured at right) stands alone near the side entrance. It is a 3-foot cast-iron piece by Michael Manzavrakos titled *South Stelae.* Seen from above it appears to be square on three sides, with a fourth side open and revealing a leaf motif.

The alliance of classical architecture and contemporary art makes a potent statement, but the result also has always struck me as very self-contained and tranquil. Somehow, I managed to frame the building within a dramatic, but almost contemplative, landscape, despite the narrow parameters of the site. When I revisit the house today, I see the old bank transformed. It reminds me of a simple Greek temple, refined and still, floating in the midst of the clamoring city.

THE NEF GARDEN

IN 1969 THE GREAT RUSSIAN-BORN FRENCH ARTIST MARC CHAGALL TOLD HIS

friends Evelyn and John Nef that he would like to give them a gift for their Georgetown

home. My neighbors the Nefs supposed he meant to give them something to display

on an inside wall. "He said he'd like to do something for our house," recalls Mrs. Nef.

They thought perhaps a small drawing. They soon learned, however, that the artist

also was a master of understatement. The planning sketch alone for the final work of

art was 3 feet wide.

Chagall's gift to the Nefs is a superb mosaic for their garden. The finished piece

measures 10 by 17 feet and was constructed in ten panels. The Nefs built a freestand-

ing wall to display it.

The Nefs' garden is an outdoor room, just 24 feet wide and 24 feet deep. I first

designed it in 1977 and then redesigned it almost twenty years later. It reflects their

history of deep friendship with the Chagalls, a rich intellectual life, and love of art.

Evelyn said, "My husband was a professor at the University of Chicago at the time.

John invited Chagall to take part in a symposium—and they found they had friends in

common. The Chagalls stayed for a time with us. He found that he could buy art sup-

plies at Woolworth's; all the neighbors were thrilled with him."

Chagall was born in 1887 in what is now Belarus. He immigrated to France in 1923, where he lived all his life, except for a several-year stint in the United States during the Nazi occupation.

The mosaic comprises thousands of tesserae or small glass and stone tiles from Carrara, in northern Italy. Some of the tiles are of natural stone; others are of brilliant gold, silver, and blue glass. The mosaic is typical of Chagall's finest work, rendering images both humorous and profound and figuring themes light and dark. Orpheus plays his lute; the three Graces dance; and the wings of Pegasus brush the sun. In the lower left-hand corner a tide of refugees appears to be crossing the sea; in the lower right, another image dear to Chagall: lovers beneath an apple tree. Chagall scholars consider this mosaic one of his most important pieces designed for private display.

Designing a garden around an important work of art presented a tremendous challenge. The garden as it now appears is a revision of my earlier design. The current plan is more ambitious than the first, with beautiful limestone tiles at the center that at night dramatically reflect the light like the surface of a pond. Benches and chairs are arranged informally beneath the trees. Other works of art inhabit the garden, including spheres by Grace Knowlton. The Nefs' backyard garden in the midst of the city integrates art and beautiful design and the richness of their way of life. "It has been the joy of the neighborhood," she says.

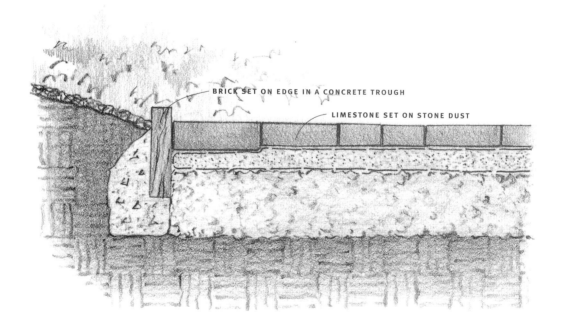

BRICK SET ON EDGE IN A CONCRETE TROUGH

LIMESTONE SET ON STONE DUST

LIMESTONE PAVING WITH BRICK EDGING

A FOUNTAIN IN NEW YORK

AT FIRST GLANCE, THIS COMMISSION MIGHT SEEM A REPETITION OF THE ONE

I had carried out for the Nefs: a city garden focusing on a wall-mounted artwork.

However, there were fundamental differences in the situation. The context of the Nef

garden had been the venerable brick town houses of Georgetown. This new garden,

by contrast, was to occupy a shallow space backing a ground floor apartment among

Manhattan's soaring mono-
liths. Morever, whereas the
Nefs had entrusted me with
framing a finished master-
piece, in this case both the art
and the garden were to be my
creation. The client's apartment was full of art—she was
a notable collector. My suggestion was that she extend this
display outdoors by backing
the garden space with a fluid
sculpture, a wall of tumbling
water that I would create.

This would serve a practical purpose in that the sound of falling water would mask intruding noises from the surrounding cityscape and so help to make the garden a true sanctuary. However, there were also compelling architectural reasons for making a water feature part of this space. This setting was one of hard-edged masonry, an unrelentingly geometrical context, and the free-form, ever-changing water would help to temper and soften that. Above all, because the garden space itself was room-sized and room-shaped, the obvious way to handle it was to integrate it with the apartment, turning the garden into an extension of the interior spaces. Art would be the common idiom that united them all.

The task of integrating apartment and garden was simplified by the fact that the two already enjoyed multiple points of connection. Entry to the garden was through a living room door, but the guest suite to the left and the dining room to the right of that also enjoyed visual access through windows. To focus the views from all of these, I chose to center the water feature on the garden's back wall, where I framed it like a painting with lush plantings.

I wanted to give the garden a floor that would seem to flow naturally out of the interior space, so I paved it with a smoothly finished, pristine terrace of limestone. This also harmonized with the limestone coping of the brick wall on which I intended to mount the water feature. I used the same limestone for this, fashioning three curvilinear shelves that I set one above the other against a limestone panel. Water is pumped to the top shelf, from which it rains down into the next and then the next shelf before falling onto the terrace floor.

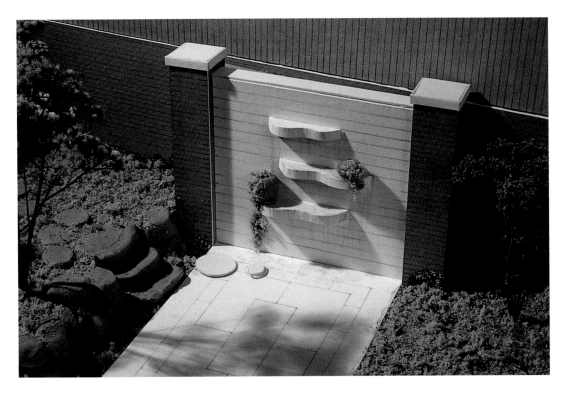

Cardboard and clay model of water feature.

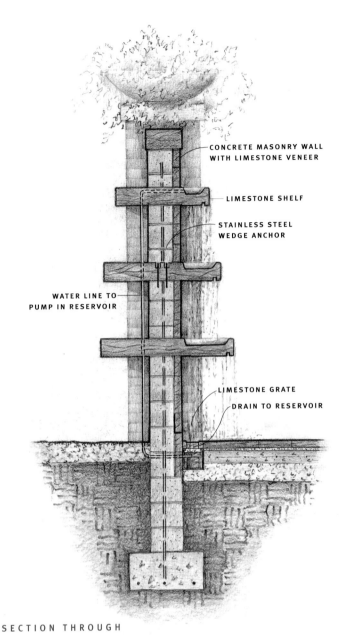

CONCRETE MASONRY WALL
WITH LIMESTONE VENEER

LIMESTONE SHELF

STAINLESS STEEL
WEDGE ANCHOR

WATER LINE TO
PUMP IN RESERVOIR

LIMESTONE GRATE
DRAIN TO RESERVOIR

SECTION THROUGH
WALL FOUNTAIN

The garden's owners wanted to avoid the maintenance that a pool would require. Instead, we let the water spill out over the pavement at the fountain's base; a channel drain collects it and carries it off to a reservoir hidden by the plantings, and from there the water is pumped back up to the fountain's top shelf. This continual wetting of the terrace at the fountain's base makes the pale limestone pavement glisten in the sunlight. At night the water reflects the lighting we installed, turning the terrace into a rippling mirror.

As I've already noted (page 37), it's especially important to use generously sized features in restricted spaces such as the garden behind this apartment. In this instance, that rule was reinforced by the fact that an urban apartment usually has only the one view (as this one did), and that view has to speak up forcefully. I used a free hand in scaling and designing this feature, so that in terms of its visual power this piece is comparable to the Nefs' mosaic. As a piece of kinetic sculpture, it extends the owners' art collection into the garden, thus linking indoors and out. Its bold, architectural simplicity is very much in tune with Manhattan. The soft murmur of the water, though, and the mask of foliage that frame it also suggest a more natural kind of place. Playing off and against the context gives this garden a special energy.

New York City's Paley Park features a "water wall" that masks city noise and brings the cooling effect of water into this scene.

chapter six

CITY LIFE ATTRACTS ME LIKE A MAGNET, BUT I'M ALSO DRAWN TO THE

country. Recently, I built a home for myself on a piece of farmland that overlooks the Chesapeake Bay (see

opposite and page 92). To get there I drive out of Washington, D.C., and across one of the world's longest sus-

pension bridges. That crossing is even longer than you might suppose, for it takes me into a different world, a

fertile countryside whose corn and soybean fields remind me of the midwestern farmlands where I grew up.

Land and sky joined by an unbroken horizon and a roadside view punctuated by hedgerows, stands of trees,

and lines of fence.

This sense of breadth only increases as I arrive at my house at the edge of the bay. As I pull in, I'm

always struck by the contrast between the setting of this new home and my familiar cityscape. I think about

that difference a lot now, for with the completion of the house I am undertaking the creation of a garden.

What I've come to recognize is that as exhilarating as the views and the sense of space may be, the land-

scape surrounding my house needs something more. It needs boundaries to contain and define these vistas. It

needs a frame to give the place its signature and a feeling of seclusion and mystery. I am just beginning to build

the garden architecture that will provide these things. It's a challenge and, perhaps surprisingly, a new experience. After all, though I've designed many country gardens for clients, I have never before faced these issues on what is literally my own turf.

TOWN OR COUNTRY?

The primary difference between creating a garden in the country and a garden in the city is, of course, one of scope. It's like the difference between writing an epic and writing a haiku. Both are poems, but one involves thousands of words, whereas the other must be completed in just seventeen syllables. The city garden measures its space in square feet, but the epic proportions of the country garden, likely to extend over acres, both simplify and complicate the country gardener's job. With more room at your disposal, you are far less limited in your options. By the same token, though, you'll find it harder to take control of a so much larger landscape. Certainly, structuring and organizing this bigger space will be more complicated.

Still, in working through the design process, the same basic rules apply. Their application changes, however, with the translation from city to country.

Begin, as usual, with the program. Ask yourself what you are going to do in this country garden. Is this to be a permanent or weekend home? If you are building a summer retreat, you may plan to eat most of your meals outside—but if you intend to spend fall and winter holidays there too, you'll want alternative facilities as well. Will you raise vegetables, flowers, and herbs, or even more substantial crops? Perhaps you'll want to include an orchard or vineyard; you may want facilities to stable a horse or house sheep or maybe chickens. Maybe your plans run more to tennis and swimming.

Will you host glamorous garden parties or entertain weekend visitors? Will you take walks through the woods or by the water's edge—or, the modern heresy, lie around and do nothing? All these dreams and plans will factor into the features you must include in the garden.

Take inventory of the surrounding natural landscape. Study the topography of the site. Take special note of natural features such as hedgerows and trees, bodies of water, and hills and valleys that you might include in your design. When working on a country garden, I always strive to link my new walls, paths, and fences with existing natural screens and boundaries. By piggybacking my architecture in this fashion, I take possession of what's already there and greatly enhance the impact of my efforts.

As always, think big.

The key to success (and fun) when building a large country garden is to relax and exploit the room you're given. Plan carefully—but don't be timid. You have more space to play with, and you can make that abundance work for you. Unlike the town garden, which must make its impression within narrow confines, the country garden can expand and tell its story in a multitude of ways.

SETTING THE STAGE

Planning such a large garden project may seem daunting at first, but a little organization and thoughtful attention to the proposed site, as the following tips illustrate, will keep the task from becoming overwhelming.

• Familiarize yourself with your site's topography. Look at the shapes created by natural field patterns; you'll want to work with these in your design. Is your site generally level, undulating, or hilly? Is there a ravine? Are there natural outcroppings of stone, rocky ledges, mounds, ditches? Is the overall topography interesting, or is it a little dull? You may feel an urge to reshape a featureless site, but don't rush into any program of regrading the terrain. It's far cheaper to work with what you've got and the results generally fit far better into the context of the surrounding countryside. Of course, you may find that certain features of your site, perhaps a steep, unstable bank or bluff near the house, present obstacles to human use or even a real hazard to users of the garden. In that case you have little choice but to adjust the terrain.

• Consider the site's other natural assets. Does it offer shoreline, wetlands, or beach? Are there ponds, lakes, or streams on the property? Stands of trees or woods?

Maybe an old meadow? Try to preserve the natural meadows and woodlands if you are fortunate to have any. Building your garden around such existing features will help it fit into the context of the surrounding landscape.

• Consider whether to keep or improve existing outbuildings such as spring houses, sheds, or barns.

• Consider local traditions when you're selecting the materials for your garden. Stone walls, for example, are characteristic of the rocky New England landscape; stone is the obvious material for paths, pavements, and other architectural features there. Wooden decking would probably be more in keeping with a seaside garden among the dunes.

• Let your garden unfold into the surrounding fields or wood. Use your plantings—hedges or screens of shrubs and trees—and hard features—walls, fences, and pergolas—like "veils." Screens and bounds are necessary for establishing and defining the garden's spaces, but they shouldn't wholly block the vision. Instead, you should be able, with a bit of effort, to see through and beyond them so that the views reveal themselves, not all at once, but slowly and by degrees.

•   In a country setting I keep the overall design as natural as possible, using sweeping curves rather than hard, rectilinear lines for architectural features such as pools, paths, and terraces.

•   Near the house I may cluster garden features such as a swimming pool, pond, terraces, and kitchen garden fairly close together. However, as the land and the viewer's eye move outward, objects should be spaced farther apart, until, like ripples in a pond, they seem to melt into the distant view.

Do your job right, and your country garden's quiet views, graceful proportions, and peacefulness should be sufficient to overcome the noisy seductions of city life—at least, I find, for a while.

A RURAL ESTATE

EVERY COUNTRY PROPERTY HAS ITS "GHOSTS"—OVERGROWN PATHS AND roads, old outbuildings, or walls or fences—and some ghosts are more insistent than others. The trick, for the designer, is to know when to honor them and when to exorcise them. In this garden I did both.

This was also a project that was complicated by the clients' conflicting goals. They had bought and restored an old farmhouse on the Eastern Shore of the Chesapeake Bay because they admired its expression of tradition, but they also felt a need to update the property so that it would accommodate their active, contemporary life.

This presented a challenge and an opportunity. I knew that the garden would have to reflect the local agricultural heritage. To work for the clients, however, it had to include a clean and efficient architectural structure. The solution I settled on was not to gloss over this difference. Instead, I chose to bond these two very different

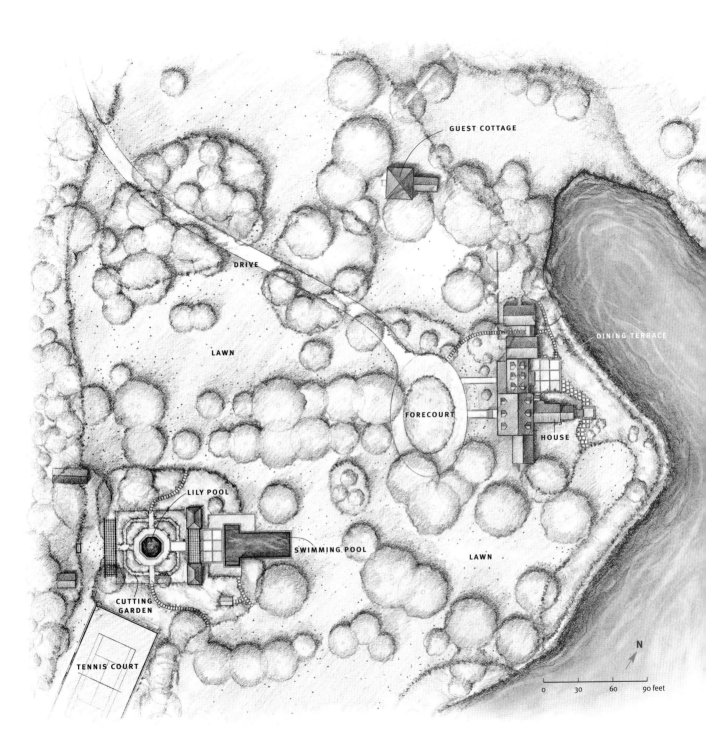

GUEST COTTAGE

DRIVE

LAWN

FORECOURT

DINING TERRACE

HOUSE

LILY POOL

SWIMMING POOL

CUTTING
GARDEN

LAWN

TENNIS COURT

N

0   30   60   90 feet

MASTER PLAN

directives together into a sort of dramatic (but carefully resolved) confrontation. I planned to do this by inlaying an elegant but functional formal garden into a soft farm landscape.

As usual, I pulled the architecture from the house, but I let the context of the landscape dictate style. Like the area around my own country home (which isn't far away), the views carried on for miles over cornfields punctuated by hedgerows and woodlots of evergreen and deciduous trees. Unlike the uninterrupted land expanses of my native Midwest, however, the Eastern Shore is characterized by a network of waterways—rivers, creeks, and brackish marshes. The wetlands teem with wildlife, especially waterfowl, and this area is a favorite stopping place on the Atlantic flyway. In spring and fall tens of thousands of geese and ducks pass overhead, large flocks often dropping down to rest from their migrations in the local fields.

This landscape is also flat and exposed. Working with it would require a mix of curves and straight lines: curves to enhance the gentler qualities of the terrain, straight lines to accommodate the geometry of the formal architectural structure I was envisioning.

My clients' house and grounds lay on a small peninsula that juts into a protected stretch of creek. That water, I found, was often calm as a millpond. Amid such tranquillity, I clearly needed to select soft-textured and soft-colored materials that would not collide with the generally soothing character of the surrounding horizontal vistas. I chose brick to construct paths, terraces, and exterior "rugs"; wood for fencing, arbors, outbuildings, and stairs; and bluestone paving and granite cobbles for other paths, terraces, and edging.

Enter the ghosts. To pay the respect to heritage that the clients desired, I could not treat this landscape as a blank slate. I had to deal with the existing drive-way approach to the house, for example. Its alignment was an unimaginative dogleg that paralleled the property line until it turned abruptly and butted up against the front door. It paid no heed to the gentle topography of the landscape, and it ensured that all night visitors would first view the house under the ugly illumination of car headlights.

There was a hint of another, older and more sensitive treatment of this approach, a ghost that survived in a meandering allée of silver maples. These trees were, alas, decrepit, beyond saving, but I realized that they traced a route that was more gracious. I restored this older alignment so that the drive once again flows in like one of the local rivers. It approaches the house off center and terminates in an ellipti-cal forecourt that I edged with stone cobbles and planted with sedum and thyme.

In re-creating the original approach to the house, however, I did not wholly erase the drive it replaced. That drive had been lined on either side by Norway maples, and I left those standing as a ghost for future generations to enjoy. If I was going to preserve this double file of trees, however, I had to make them work as part of the new design. I did this by resurfacing the track between them with turf and using the result-ing shaded walkway as a path from house to swimming pool. In this context the angu-lar geometry of the route was an advantage, for it reinforced the formal tone of the gardens I planned around the pool.

The landscape immediately around the house was my next concern. It faced the creek on two sides and incorporated wetland areas as well as lawn. I set to work behind the house by removing two massive unkempt holly trees. By blocking light and air, they kept the area adjoining the back of the house unpleasantly damp and dark.

After letting in the sun, I invited the host and hostess and their guests out. I did this by setting a brick terrace at the foot of a flight of wood steps that lead out from the dining room. A trail of stepping stones connects the dining terrace with another brick pavement, a terrace adjoining the gun room. Between the terraces and the creek's bank, I brushed in sweeps of perennials and ornamental grasses, to add visual drama to the scene and also to help control soil erosion (see page 103).

Returning to the front of the house, I began placing the swimming pool and its accompanying gardens. Farthest from the house, at the southwest corner of the front lawn, I installed a vegetable and cut-flower garden. This was designed to be ornamental as well as utilitarian. An octagonal lily pool surrounded by a heavy limestone cop-

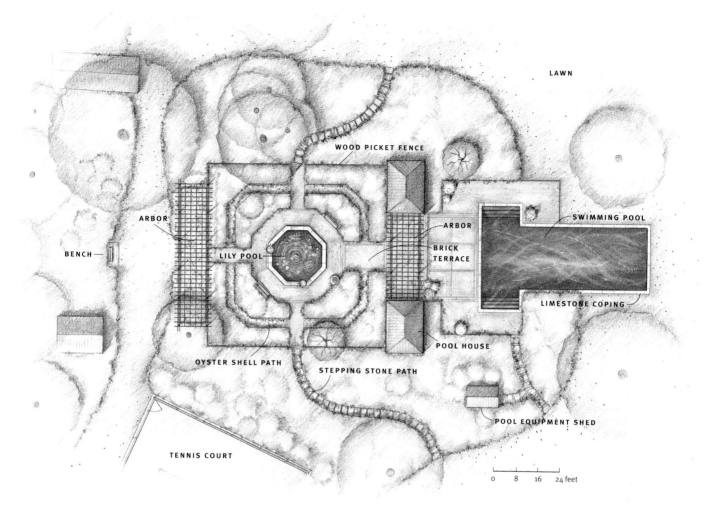

LAWN

WOOD PICKET FENCE

ARBOR

BENCH

LILY POOL

ARBOR

BRICK TERRACE

SWIMMING POOL

LIMESTONE COPING

OYSTER SHELL PATH

STEPPING STONE PATH

POOL HOUSE

POOL EQUIPMENT SHED

TENNIS COURT

0   8   16   24 feet

SWIMMING POOL TERRACE AND CUTTING GARDEN

ing became the central focus of this working garden; paths of oystershell (a traditional paving material around the Chesapeake) radiate out from the pool to define a pattern of geometric beds.

I bracketed this garden with arbors and enclosed it with a white picket fence. Bounding the side nearest to the house are a pair of twin pool houses, built to serve the swimming pool. The generous dimensions of the pool, 22 by 66 feet, make it an important feature of the landscape. I swathed it in a profusion of herbs, perennials, and grasses to soften the architecture's hard edges and corners and to ease the transition to the informal countryside all around. At the same time, though, I emphasized the striking formality of the pool. I pargeted its inner surface black to enhance the reflective quality of the water. It's a mirror now, a framed patch of sky caught and held at the garden's heart.

Sunlight flickers on all of this: pool, pond, and river. This common element unifies the scene while also drawing attention to its contrasts. You discover drama in the midst of repose here, new conveniences integrated with old beauties. Ghosts haunt this place still, but who would have it any other way?

THE TOWN GARDEN

chapter seven

P ARADOX IS THE ESSENCE OF THE TOWN GARDEN AND THE
key to its special appeal. Such a quiet plot of earth is extraordinarily precious when set in the midst
of a bustling city. It's a scrap of nature that is somehow made to seem all the wilder by surrounding
vistas of tall buildings. Still, precious as the town garden may be, it's typically characterized by an
impoverished soil and a scarcity of sunlight. Somehow, though, these limitations make the fruits of
the urban oasis all the more delightful.

I speak of these particular challenges and pleasures with special feeling, for they have
long been part of my daily routine. For thirty years I have lived in a narrow town house in the
Georgetown district of Washington, D.C. Set behind the house is a scrap of a garden just 17 feet
wide and 55 feet deep. I've turned this into an extension of my home, a roofless room that brings a
welcome sense of space into an otherwise tightly architected dwelling. The garden has also been
an opportunity for self-expression, a work of art that alters chameleon-like with the weather and
the seasons. It has been an experimental stage on which my friends and I have acted out many
parts over the years. It's also, quite simply, one of my favorite views in the world.

Building and maintaining a garden in town demands exceptional discipline. In the town garden every inch counts, and every choice you make becomes a significant gesture. As a town gardener you'll also need a sense of humor, for to succeed in this venture you must be willing to experiment, and your experiments will bring setbacks as well as successes.

Whatever you do in a town garden, you soon run up against the spatial limitations of the site. Treat these as a challenge and an opportunity; by playing with and against the limitations, you can extend the pleasures of your garden. In his professional memoir, *The Education of a Gardener,* famous English garden designer Russell Page wrote that the small garden plot at the heart of a city appears at first glance to pose "an almost hopeless problem." But, he added, just by shifting our point of view, we can achieve remarkable results. On town plots, he explained, "One has to garden by allusion." A few carefully chosen and placed rocks may suggest a mountainside; a few fistfuls of grasses introduce a memory of the meadow. Imaginative use of colors and material is essential here, and you must keep a firm grasp of scale and proportion. In your town garden, there's no room for false notes or empty gestures.

When I undertake the demanding (but exciting) job of designing a town garden, I find it helpful to keep in mind the following:

• Space in town gardens is precious; make effective use of every square inch.

• A garden should be an extension of the house. This is especially true in an urban setting, where the interior space is likely to be limited too. Consider carefully how you can make your town garden an extension of the house and an outdoor living room.

• If you think of your town garden as just another room in the house, your building materials must be chosen accordingly, and using a little sleight of hand to promote

the illusion of continuity also is important. I like to pull the floor of the room adjacent

into the garden floor if possible. I know of an example in which the interior floor was

painted in trompe l'oeil to resemble the Pennsylvania bluestone terrace outside. This

was done so cleverly that it was almost impossible to distinguish one from the other.

•	You may find, as I have, that your town garden is as important for the view it

provides as for its living space. My Georgetown garden is an extension of my kitchen.

However, I rarely sit out on the small 7-by-17-foot terrace just beyond the double

French doors. Instead, I sit in the kitchen and look out as though viewing a painting or

sculpture. Of course, many people who live in the city do use their gardens for their

meals or to relax, but I prefer to enjoy it as a view rather than inhabit it as a room.

Along the same lines, because a small town garden often is the main view to the out-

doors from your house, it must be done right. I say to clients, "This is your view of

the sea or the mountains, so don't skimp. Give this space drama and mystery and

let it change throughout the year—because you are going to be looking at it every day."

• Be adventurous in your choice of plants. Because the temperature in a city is often a few degrees higher than that of the surrounding countryside, a small garden in town will often safely host species that won't survive a few miles away out in the suburbs. The temperature in my town garden commonly registers 10 degrees warmer than those reported from areas beyond city limits.

• Look for borrowed scenery. Large or small, the town garden must take advantage of whatever landmarks are in sight—a church steeple or a neighbor's tree, for example. Take possession of these views by including some echo, of form, color, or materials, in your own garden.

• Of course, external views may also be a liability. Who wants to gaze out at the air-conditioning condenser on the neighbor's roof or, as my friend does, the sign for a funeral home? These less desirable views may be obscured using trellises, vines, a new tree, or a shrub.

• Create mystery in your town garden. I do this by layering space, that is, by using garden structures and plants to hide and then gradually reveal parts of the garden as you move through it. By imposing many experiences one on the other, you create the impression that the garden has much more depth than it actually does. This layering can be done with a variety of elements, such as trellises, arbors, walls, paving patterns, sculpture, gazebos, and fencing, in addition to furniture and, of course, plantings.

• Create drama. In my garden I used the natural downward slope of the land from the rear fence line to the house to create the illusion of a theatrical set, with a raked or inclined stage. When I'm in the kitchen looking out, a cat sitting in the middle of the path looks as impressive as a lion.

• Light and shadow play particularly important roles in a town garden. In a small space, daily and seasonal shifts in light convey significant changes in mood, and your garden can appear quite different from one moment to the next. Use these shifts of light and shadow to increase your garden's mystery or influence its character. I talk more about using artificial lighting on page 233, but especially in the town garden, artificial light is essential, whatever the season. In particular, this treatment will do more than any other design technique to extend the interior of your house into the outdoors.

I find lighting especially important in my town garden in winter when the glass doors are closed. Focusing the lights upward into the trees creates enchanting effects, and there is nothing more beautiful than light reflecting off snow at night. Use your garden illumination like the foot- and spotlights of a theater to enhance the power and drama of your open-air stage. After all, why should you let the curtain fall on your garden with sunset? You deserve a better performance than that.

THE SULLIVAN GARDEN

GEORGETOWN IS THE OLDEST NEIGHBORHOOD IN WASHINGTON, D.C. IT WAS a busy, prosperous seaport in its own right before the Founding Fathers established a national capital. With its tree-shaded blocks of old brick town houses, it still preserves the intimacy of a small Southern city, even though it is just minutes from Capitol Hill. Many of the homes date back to the Revolutionary War or before. From the street these houses give very little away. Indeed, these well-bred and well-kept dowagers present very similar faces.

Once you get past the front door, however, the impression of sameness ends. I never know what to expect when I enter one of the Georgetown homes for a first meeting with a client. The Sullivan home is a case in point. The facade may be buttoned-down Georgian brick, but the interior of the house has been transformed by the owners' passionate connection to Haitian art. The rooms speak of humor and taste— clearly, there's nothing stuffy or straitlaced about the Sullivans.

The house's interior was also utterly unlike the backyard, which remained as

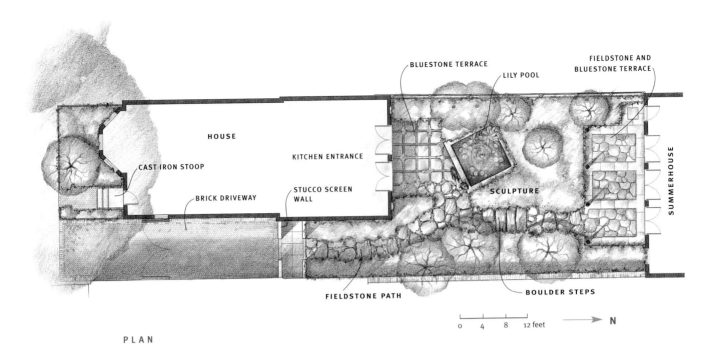

BLUESTONE TERRACE

LILY POOL

FIELDSTONE AND
BLUESTONE TERRACE

HOUSE

KITCHEN ENTRANCE

CAST IRON STOOP

STUCCO SCREEN
WALL

SCULPTURE

BRICK DRIVEWAY

SUMMERHOUSE

FIELDSTONE PATH

BOULDER STEPS

0   4   8   12 feet   N

PLAN

everly and John Sullivan had found it when they bought the house. A previous owner

had paved the whole space with concrete and backed it with a three-bay garage.

Inside the house I found two indications of what sort of garden would please

my new clients. The first was the art. Mr. Sullivan is an enthusiastic collector. Mrs.

Sullivan's interest is professional and personal—in addition to collecting modern and

traditional Haitian painting and sculpture for herself, she is also an active dealer. Her

finds cover the walls, in some places all the way from floor to ceiling. The feast of tex-

tures and colors might well be overwhelming, if they weren't contained by the temper-

ing frame of the house's formal Georgian architecture. It struck me, though, that the

display needed to expand. This, I decided, would be a case in which I would pull not

only the architecture but also the art from the house. I soon came to visualize the gar-

den as a sort of outdoor theater in which the players would be the artworks.

I also found a clue about what sort of garden would suit the Sullivans in the character of their kitchen. I'm always interested in how clients organize and decorate their homes, and I'm particularly interested in kitchens, as today that's so often the focal point of family life. It's the room, I've found, where people express themselves most openly. In this home the kitchen was especially relevant to the garden's design. Like most town houses, this one had been built on a relatively long and narrow plan with the kitchen set at the rear, serving as the only access from house to backyard.

With its wood floor and Oriental rug, the Sullivan kitchen was obviously the most lived-in room of the house. Organized in the round, the kitchen had a fireplace along one curve, a couple of rocking chairs, open shelves, built-in cabinetry, warm

lighting, and generous areas for cooking and working. The large round table at the center serves as both formal and informal dining space and worktable. The room is the true hearth of the house.

Two sets of French doors provided access from kitchen to backyard, so this area could easily become an extension of the central living space right through every season except perhaps winter. Even when the weather was truly inhospitable, they'd have a view to enjoy.

I framed that transition with a clematis-covered arbor, which extends over the kitchen door. To blur the passage from indoors to out, I surfaced the area right outside those French doors with a stone floor neatly bordered by flagstones. At the far edge of that I set a rectilinear lily pool on the bias. This represented a compromise: the Sullivans wanted to incorporate water into the design but didn't want the trouble of caring for a swimming pool. The lily pool, incidentally, provided a perfect site for a favorite work of art. On the pool edge sits a simple cement statue of a woman by Mary Brownstein. From spring through fall this serene, contemplative figure is swathed in tall grasses. In midwinter it poses stark, alone except for an attentive dog, also modeled from concrete.

A triangular area, overflowing with coreopsis, liatris, and drifts of Russian sage in summertime, intervenes between the pool and the flight of steps that leads up to the garden's next level. A tall hedge of bamboo stands to the right, and the niches I found in an existing brick garden wall are now set with antique Haitian water jars.

The steps leading up from the pool take the visitor to an arbor-covered terrace. An echo of the arbor over the kitchen door, this one frames the front of the garden house. This was created by adapting the existing garage; it now serves for storage but could easily function as an office, another dining room, or even a small art gallery. Its access, like that of the kitchen, is through a series of French doors that can be folded back to erase the division between in and out.

In any case, the upper terrace adjoining this structure is a special place. The terrace floor here is stone too, though of a more rustic character than that next to the house. Here, inside the enclosing border of bluestone, the pavement is pieced together from randomly shaped fieldstones. The arbor casts wonderful striped shadows in winter, and in summer overflows with clematis vines, foliage, and blossoms—outsized purple blooms of *Clematis x jackmanii* stirred into the clouds of tiny white fragrant flowers borne by *Clematis terniflora*. The area beneath this trellis is also

paved in stone, but stone of a
more rustic character.

When I return periodi-
cally for a visit, I find the garden being enjoyed fully and
put to use in all the ways the
Sullivans had dreamed of. The
architecture of this town garden has given the Sullivans
a tremendous framework for
extending their passion for art
into nature.

THE SIMMONS GARDEN

ANOTHER APPROACH TO DESIGNING A GARDEN FOR A TIGHT URBAN SPACE IS to create a very formal plan. This garden also promised to furnish a particularly appropriate complement to the Simmons home, an early-nineteenth-century town house in Old Town, Alexandria, Virginia. Furnished with magnificent early American antiques, the house has an air of great polish, and no visible "loose ends." The garden, designed to accompany this handsome dwelling, reflects a nineteenth-century attention to order and rationality. To achieve this effect I had to make every detail, every feature count, but the net result was an atmosphere that is serene and meditative. The garden is also a superb space for entertaining.

The areas to be designed included a front yard (opposite page), side yard, and backyard. By using careful detailing with each element designed in scale with a very tight space, I was able to include many features normally found only in larger properties. Despite the location in a city center, for example, I found room in the back garden for a swimming pool, a spa, and an elaborate arbor, which links the main house to an old carriage house at the rear of the property.

Integrating all these elements of the back garden was a special challenge because that area encompassed three levels. From a back porch you descend six

steps to an intermediate level or mezzanine, from which three more steps take you down at last to the swimming pool and its accompanying terrace. The arbor provides shade in summer, and, by screening the view of the pool terrace from the second-floor windows of neighboring houses, it also ensures privacy.

I redesigned the existing swimming pool to function as a lap pool, and at night it becomes a gorgeous reflecting pool. Water jets located on either side can be switched on to form an arch of water that falls in the pool's center. A small spa at the far end, next to the carriage house, serves as a terminus for the arbor. Each element—pool, spa, carriage house, arbor—connects the small garden space to the main house, everything tied together visually by a series of low stone walls. The arbor's slats are closely spaced so that they create interesting shadows during the day and at night when the garden is lit. This garden reminds me of a Japanese garden in its quiet, orderly simplicity—every detail speaks.

I encouraged the Simmonses to develop the space in the front and side yards as their own and not to treat it as a public space, as people who live in a town house so often do. The front garden proved large enough for a terrace and generous planting. What a luxury for a city dweller, to be able to entertain in front of the house—and also to have a lovely view of the planting from the living room windows. The side garden terrace, which opens off the family room, furnishes additional space in which to entertain. I made the plantings here, which include a magnolia and crape myrtles, deliberately dramatic to catch the eye and help screen what's going on in the garden from the street.

Coordinating all these different elements involved drawing on the best of several gardening traditions. Ultimately, though, by including all the various features, by making them all work together, I achieved a design of extraordinary depth and one that permits a range of uses unusual in a town garden.

THE MOORE GARDEN

DIVIDING THE GARDEN INTO DISTINCT ROOMS CAN
be an effective and appealing way to organize a rural
landscape. In the city this treatment may be a necessity.
The compact size of city gardens means the competing
uses are more likely to interfere with each other, unless
the space is carefully and clearly structured. That, certainly, was the case with the
Moore garden, a design I developed for the owners of a historic house in the center of
Washington, D.C. When successful, such a design offers more than just freedom for all
to pursue personal interests. By fitting a number of different experiences into the
available space, it greatly increases its apparent size.

Both Robert and Mary Moore wanted an outdoor dining space, so I designed a
room for that purpose, setting it in the obvious spot, right outside the kitchen. Mrs.
Moore maintained an office at home and wanted to expand that space. For her I created an open-air conference room. Communicating directly with the office, this outdoor extension would provide a unique facility for meetings through three seasons of
the year in Washington's mild climate.

The Moores' four children needed room for play, and we gave them two rooms. One, an area stretching across the rear of the property, offered a lawn appropriate for rugby. The other play space was one that the children would have to share with the adults, a room with a swimming pool and sunning terrace. To satisfy Mr. Moore's interest in gardening, I hedged the sports lawn with flower borders so that he would have room to grow his favorite flowers and herbs.

The challenge of a design of this sort is that the rooms, while functioning on their own as discrete spaces, should also pull together as a whole. There must be a sense of unity so that the garden reads as a single composition.

We achieved this in part by keeping the transitions from room to room distinct

but relatively subtle. I designed each room to rest on a different level. To enter each, you either rise or descend a couple of steps. To establish a unifying theme, I installed brick or stone carpets in each room—but I changed the paving pattern from room to room to give each one its own identity. I also varied the plantings from room to room to accommodate and enhance the intended use and scale of each.

A useful rule for town gardens, I have found, is that the more intimate the space you are working with, the more intricate and detailed the planting design and architecture should be. In this case, I used containers and furniture to add to the atmosphere of each garden room. In the dining room, where a note of elegance was wanted, I installed a bronze fountain with Etruscan overtones by sculptor John Dreyfuss. This gives that space an original and very bold focal point, and the fountain's air of antiquity matches the historic character of the house.

I deliberately applied a dense combination of elements to the Moore garden, and the powerful interplay of textures, colors, and materials creates a rich mood. Wood, brick, exquisite cabinetry and sculpture, and the subtle use of lighting have made this a vivid, protected world, one that belies the garden's site in the heart of the city.

THE SEASIDE GARDEN

IGREW UP ON THE SHORE OF AN INLAND SEA, THE GREAT LAKE Michigan, and in the winter my parents took me to the Florida coast, where my father kept a simple fishing boat. We often spent days together fishing out in the Gulf of Mexico. At the new house I have built by the Chesapeake Bay, water and open sky once again surround me. It's a setting in which I feel very much at home.

The beach is a powerful and uncompromising landscape. The dramatic horizontal views are vast and overwhelming. The lines where the water meets the sky and where the land meets water are sharply drawn. The rough music of waves and wind are constants, the water is always in motion. This is a wild place, one that has always filled me with a sense of discovery and anticipation.

Seaside gardens—the good ones—have an austere, subtle beauty, and their bones should correspond. Consider the classic seaside path: a boardwalk made of slats of wood, a narrow track, weathered gray, set atop the dunes. Simple, easy to replace, beautiful.

To create a garden by the sea involves special challenges. To begin with, it's difficult to come to terms with the sweeping vistas. In *The Education of a Gardener,* Russell Page wrote, "If I were to choose a garden for myself I would prefer a hollow to a hilltop. A panorama and a garden seen together distract from each other. One's interest is torn between the garden pattern with its shapes and colours in the foreground and the excitement of the distant view." Although I disagree with his conclusion—I like the challenge presented by a panoramic view—I concur with his presentation of the problem. That is the difficulty of designing a seaside garden: instead of trying to compete with the sublime view, you must frame and draw attention to it. At the same time, you must also provide some seclusion and privacy and a firm, personal sense of place. In short, the seaside

garden must include areas both exposed and private, areas that present the mighty view and areas that protect us from it.

Page always insisted that the site should "tell its own story." On that point I am in complete agreement. Less powerful settings may clamor for definition; the architect, through his additions, creates the sense of place. When you are by the sea, however, you always know where you are. A seaside site can speak for itself, and architecture that calls attention to itself, through complicated design details or grandiose materials, merely seems impertinent. This is something the Japanese have long understood. They don't crowd their coastal gardens with ornaments. Instead, they keep the focus on the sea and treat the garden as a vantage point for viewing.

When designing a seaside garden, I follow the Japanese masters' example and keep the architecture uncomplicated. My task, as I see it, is to preserve the dramatic view, connect the house with its site, and protect it from wind and salt. I try to inject some domesticity. I'm likely, for example, to frame the view with a foreground that establishes a more human sense of scale and proportion. The walls, trellises, or pergolas I use to accomplish this also create the kind of layering I referred to in my rules for the city garden (pages 110–13). As magnificent as the seaside view may be, you don't want to reveal it all at once, or your garden will have no depth. Why squander all the excitement of the site on one moment?

The edge where the garden meets the natural landscape is always important, and in a seaside setting it must be handled with special care. You need to mark the transition, but, as I have said, you don't want to compete with the scenery beyond. Keep the edge unobtrusive. A low, undulating wall along the terrace edge, for instance, will furnish the sense of enclosure you need without intruding on the drama of the view. Setting a sculpture off to one side of a garden area also frames the view and helps define the space without dominating it.

I've mentioned the need to domesticate the garden, but be careful not to make it too cozy. The proportions and dimensions of a seaside garden must be generous, if it isn't to be overwhelmed by the vastness beyond. This applies not only to paths and fences but to garden structures as well, from summerhouses and follies to pergolas, porches, decks, and storage buildings.

The seaside, with its intense sunlight, sandy soil, constant wind, and salt spray, is a hostile environment for many plants. The plants that thrive here tend to be

those whose colors are muted—like heather and the gray-green lavenders, santolinas, and grasses. Though not lush, these plants have interesting textures and they possess another outstanding virtue: they like a seaside habitat.

Take your clue from the flora when selecting building materials. These too should be simple and durable. Textures may be rugged but colors should be subdued—the colors of your architecture should complement rather than compete with the colors in the landscape. This is why in a seaside setting I particularly like to work in wood. It weathers well to a silvery gray that harmonizes with the colors of beach and sea. Because the wind-driven sand and salt are hard on seaside architecture, I use only the toughest woods, timbers such as redwood, pressure-treated pine, and cypress, to construct seaside walls, decks, and planters. For steps and retaining walls, I prefer to use railroad ties.

Some of the materials and colors I most favor for seaside gardens come from the landscape itself. Although I use the architecture to delineate the frontier between garden and surrounding beach, I also have fun constructing it in such a way as to gently blur that boundary. I still use stone or wood for pool terraces and walkways in my seaside gardens, but I'm just as likely to choose sand-colored gravel or, better still, crushed shell for those driveways and paths. Even though I may follow a formal design tradition, I'll treat it more playfully. I might mow a meadow to create the suggestion of a parterre. Working found objects from the beach—driftwood, shells, and seaglass—into the architectural framework also brings the garden closer to that mysterious sea edge.

SHORT POINT FARM

SHORT POINT FARM IS AN ENTIRE WORLD where sea and land meet in intimate partnership. This 85-acre estate was nothing like that, however, when the owner first called me for assistance. He knew the potential was there. He had fallen in love with this wild parcel and its setting on a peninsula along Rhode Island's Narragansett Bay. The new owner bought the land to preserve it, and he was determined to preserve it not only as a place for people—a weekend home for his family—but also as a sanctuary for the native flora and wildlife.

Although the landscape was overgrown with tangled vines, brush, and weeds, the combination of forest, meadow, and rocky coastline created a dynamic, seductive mood. My job, like that of a gem cutter, would not be to change this jewel but rather to remove the nonessentials and reveal the grace and beauty within. Our goal would be

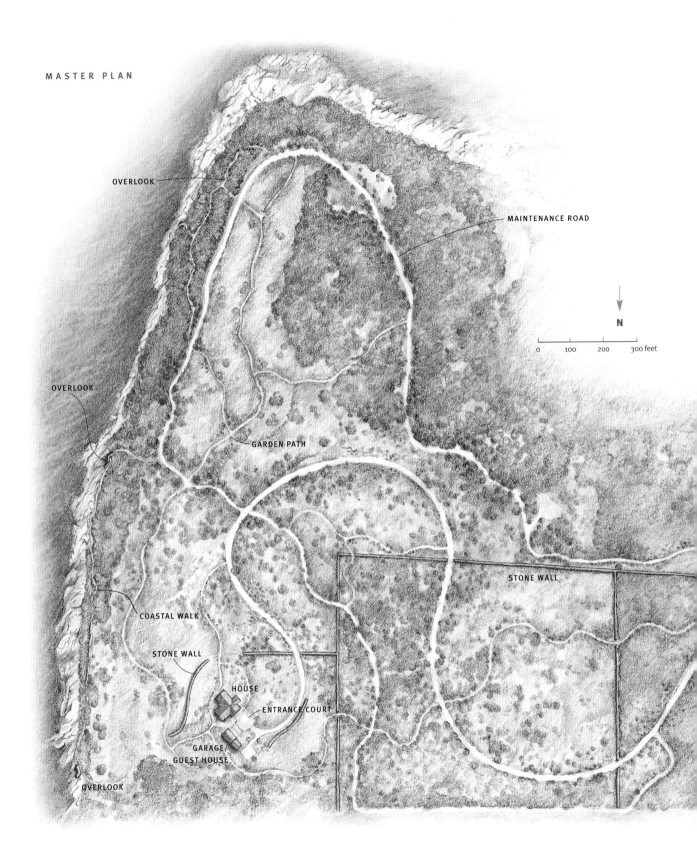

OVERLOOK

MAINTENANCE ROAD

N

0   100   200   300 feet

OVERLOOK

GARDEN PATH

STONE WALL

COASTAL WALK

STONE WALL

HOUSE

ENTRANCE COURT

GARAGE/
GUEST HOUSE

OVERLOOK

to unveil the landscape's inherent qualities without essentially altering them.

It is easy to become overwhelmed by a property this size. You don't know where to start, especially when you are so anxious not to put your wrong foot forward. The safest approach is the one that we decided to follow in this case: spend time getting to know the place, and then allow its character to guide the design decisions.

I walked the site many times with my client, learning its contours, liabilities, and assets. We began to clear the land of unwanted undergrowth, taking our time and cutting selectively so that the magnificent red cedars and junipers were preserved. At the same time, we began to carve walking paths throughout the property, creating a complex of paths so meticulously fitted to the landscape that they looked as old as the trees among which they were woven. This first step of the design process took more than a year.

Ruins of old New England stone walls that once delineated the countryside lay in the fields and woodlands. This was a fortunate legacy. I was able to reuse all of this stone to create low walls that give the landscape its definition and establish a sense of place, even before the owner had sited the house. This choice of materials, incidentally, became a precedent for the rest of the project. Whatever we built thereafter, we used understated, earthy, and durable materials that harmonized with the natural character of the site.

Having carved out a framework of paths and laid out a framework of walls, I began to fill in the blanks, working out the

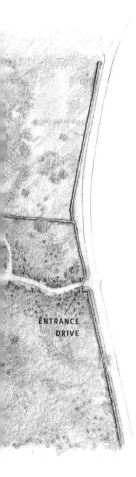

ENTRANCE
DRIVE

character of the various spaces. A cedar gate set in restored stone walls marked

the entrance to the property; from this a drive wound through a series of different

landscapes toward a gradual discovery of the sea.

That feature isn't apparent to any of the senses as you enter the landscape closest to the front gate. Here you find a 9-acre inland meadow of native plants, surrounded by the semidry laid stone walls. These are low but stout, 24 inches high, 15 inches wide at the top, and slightly wider at the base. After passing through this

grassland, the drive winds through another gate—a gap in the wall, really—and into an inland forest of mature cedars. Here the first hint of the salt breeze is apparent; and with their splendid trunks freed of vines and undergrowth, those cedars stand like sentries on the floor of mown turf.

Beyond the cedar forest, delineated by another boundary of walls, lie the seaside meadow and woodland. You'll find the first views of bay and ocean here, and if you wander through the net of paths that weaves together the trees and grasses, you'll eventually arrive right at the sea's edge.

The final landscape, the one nearest the house, is a complex of perennial gardens and paved terraces of bluestone and granite cob-

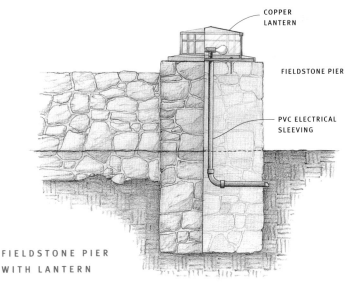

COPPER
LANTERN

FIELDSTONE PIER

PVC ELECTRICAL
SLEEVING

FIELDSTONE PIER
WITH LANTERN

bles. The views from here are extraordinary: north across Narragansett Bay to the Newport Harbor and skyline, east to the Atlantic Ocean, and southeast to Block Island in the far distance. However, the shore remains out of reach: a low, S-shaped wall divides the garden from the 200-foot scrub buffer (required by coastal zone management laws) that lines the water's edge.

For access to the water, I designed three lookout points over the rocky cliffs.

Into the shale escarpment below I fitted stairs made of mahogany, a boatbuilder's timber that can withstand the salt spray of the breaking sea. These zigzag down the 70 feet to water's edge. Both lookout and stairs were crafted with a shipwright's care. Constructed with marine hardware, these structures are secured with metal stays like those of a sailboat.

Such details were typical of the quiet but sturdy purposefulness of the entire design. From the big picture down to the level of minute detail, the plan I arrived at was simple and functional, and it dovetailed perfectly with the land it occupied. Thanks to the owner's passionate enthrallment with the land—he's a conservationist to the core—I was able to focus here on rejuvenating it rather than reshaping it to

meet unrealistic demands. Today this seaside retreat is a place to walk and contemplate, a place where the variety of habitats supports a diversity of wildlife, where ribbons of stones thread through the trees in a salute to old New England.

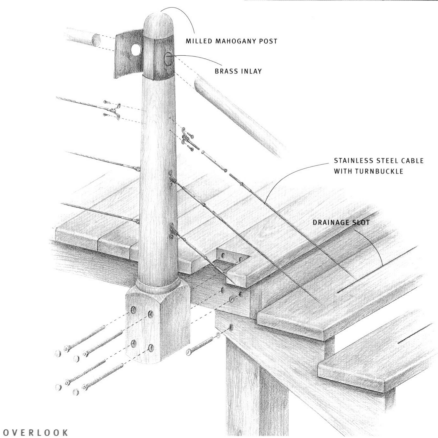

MILLED MAHOGANY POST

BRASS INLAY

STAINLESS STEEL CABLE
WITH TURNBUCKLE

DRAINAGE SLOT

OVERLOOK

AN ISLAND RETREAT

IF I WERE ABLE TO DESIGN MY OWN client, the mistress of this Carolina Low Country retreat might serve as the model. A woman with a keen sense of style, she collects contemporary craftsman furniture—one-of-a-kind creations that have transformed familiar domestic objects into the expressions of an artistic vision. She understands and loves fine workmanship.

Certainly, this landscape presented challenges. The setting was magnificent: an 85-acre island that had been part of an old rice plantation on the South Carolina coast. Palmettos mixed with live oaks and other subtropical hardwoods in dense and tangled woodland; edging these were the seemingly endless expanses of salt marsh and abandoned paddies that now were home to wood storks and alligators. The "Low Country" is what the locals call their home. Floods are common here, and my clients'

house had to be set up on 8-foot pilings to elevate it above the projected worst-case high-water mark. Indeed, to identify potential views, my clients and I had to use stepladders to mimic what the perspective would be from the house.

Marrying this house to the land was going to involve some bridge building, and this had to be done sensitively. The community to which the island belongs is committed to the preservation of the local habitat. Its codes dictate that disturbance of the natural landscape be minimal and that native species only be used in the planting.

The architect for the house, William McDonough, embraced the concerns of the community wholeheartedly and designed the house as a sort of sophisticated tropical camp. The buildings were dispersed into a service complex (with garage, workshop, and generator) and the main house, which was to be approached by a long drive that wound through the trees or by foot through the great meadow that I created—a quilt of native grasses and wildflowers. The footpath was carefully directed both to present users with a succession of choice views and to divert them around the slough on whose bank Judy, a 6-foot alligator, likes to bask.

The clients and their architect chose a Japanese-inspired style for the house, one that emphasizes meticulous joinery and a rich palette of indigenous woods. The rooms are timbered with oak and paneled with butternut hickory and pine; the exterior walls are sheathed in cedar and the columns that support the encircling verandah are turned from massive logs of "sunken" cypress. Sunken cypress is an almost archaeological material, first-growth cypress trunks that sank to the bottom of the trees' native swamps during the logging drives of the last century. Impervious to rot, the submerged cypress wood has remained sound while acquiring a special luster and is eagerly sought now by exacting woodworkers.

Opposite: Interior courtyard.

To marry the high-stepping house with the low-lying land around it, I decided to surround the base of the house with a stepped series of decks. In this way, the house would seem to grow up out of the plain, rather than perching on it. Wood was the obvious choice of materials because it would pull out the architecture of the house. The location also dictated its use. The sea is all around; wind and wind-born spray are a constant. As with other seaside gardens, wood is the building material best equipped to survive this sort of environmental assault and one that becomes even more beautiful as it weathers. Finally, I also felt that wood was best suited to this design because of the community's insistence that house and garden must integrate with the setting. Handsome as it is, timber is an unassuming material, one that tends to complement a landscape rather than compete with it.

The wood I specified for the decking is *danto,* a tropical timber that is harvested on a renewable basis. In keeping with my clients' love of craftsmanship, I paid special attention to the joinery; as with the house, I drew on the Japanese tradition for

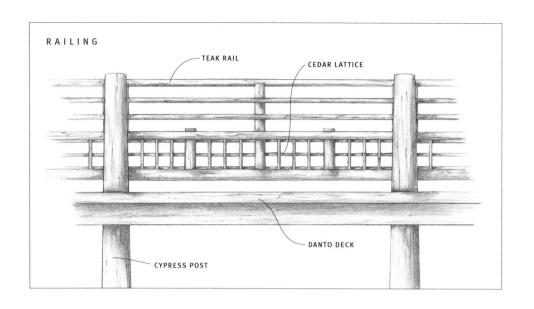

RAILING

TEAK RAIL

CEDAR LATTICE

DANTO DECK

CYPRESS POST

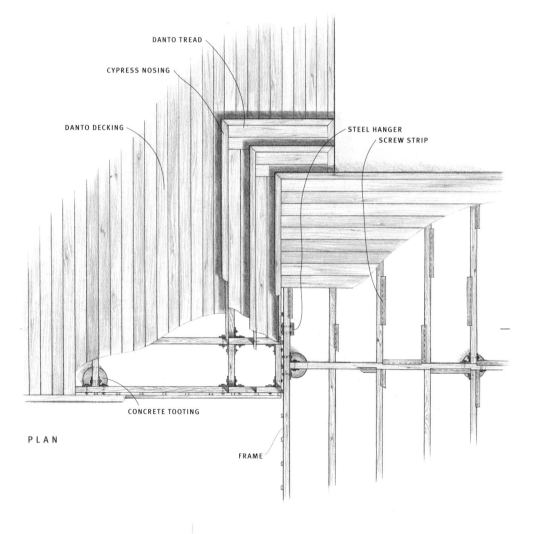

DANTO TREAD

CYPRESS NOSING

DANTO DECKING

STEEL HANGER
SCREW STRIP

CONCRETE TOOTING

PLAN

FRAME

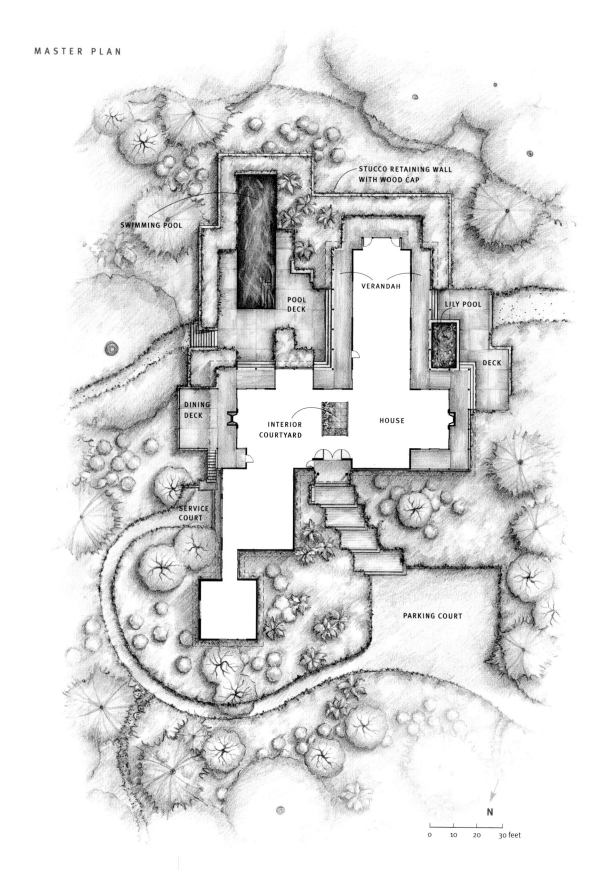

STUCCO RETAINING WALL
WITH WOOD CAP

SWIMMING POOL

POOL
DECK

VERANDAH

LILY POOL

DECK

DINING
DECK

INTERIOR
COURTYARD

HOUSE

SERVICE
COURT

PARKING COURT

N

0   10   20   30 feet

the detailing. Corners are mitered, lapped, or dovetailed. As my clients happily noted, the whole garden is built like a piece of furniture. Scale is managed as carefully as the carpentry—decks, steps, and copings are proportioned, to bring you up to the house or down to the land gracefully.

The architecture of this island garden is restful. It rises from the land in broad, natural-seeming tiers. Native plants complement the semitropical structures and reinforce the environmentally friendly character of the design. The decks seem to float on a sea of grass and meadow flowers, mirroring the horizon that stretches beyond the reef. Everything here feels crafted and permanent, but it retains the resting-lightly-on-the-land mood of a seaside encampment.

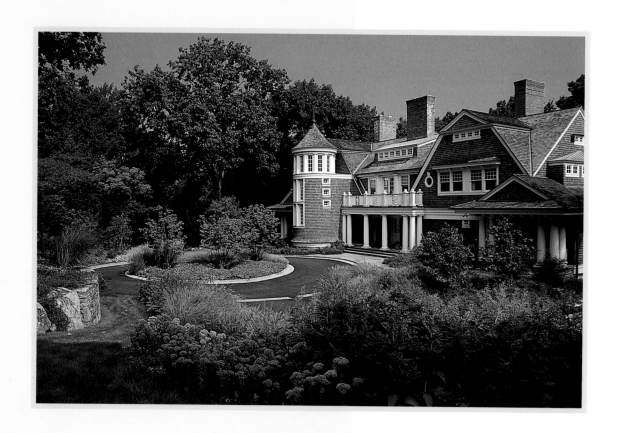

A GARDEN BY THE SHORE

MY DESIGN FOR THE FOLLOWING PROPERTY, A 9-ACRE ESTATE OVERLOOKING New York's Long Island Sound, started with a resolve to work with, and build on, the unique qualities of a remarkable site.

The center point of my design had to be, of course, the clients' 10,000-square-foot country mansion. Given the unusual attractions of the setting, though, I felt it was essential that the house should come to seem part of the landscape rather than dominating it. In particular, despite the dwelling's imposing presence, I wanted to focus

the views outward, toward the soft meadows and salt marshes and the sea beyond. At

the same time, however, I wanted to retain a feeling of intimacy in the areas of the gar-

den close to the house.

The final design ties the house to the land through various terraces and steps,

capitalizing on the natural changes in grade. Through this I also extended the interior

living space outdoors, turning the various levels of the garden into open-air rooms for

entertaining and relaxing. Alternately grand and private, these rooms offer a succes-

sion of different experiences, though in a less linear form than the Georgetown gar-

den's "progressive informality" (see page 115).

The principal sequence of rooms in my design began with a porch terrace (see page 155) that extends the living space from the back of the house. Here I played with the pattern of the paving, creating three distinct stone rugs to divide the terrace into different spaces for use in entertaining or enjoying the view. A wing at either end of the house flanks this area, and I installed stone planters filled with flowering perennials and cascading shrubs to further embrace it and give it, despite its grand view, the feeling of intimacy I sought.

From the porch terrace, turfed steps bordered in granite cobbles descend to a broad, curvilinear terrace of lawn over-looking the sound. This space I framed with a stone border and masses of ornamental perennials and grasses. Below this, down an additional 20-foot descent, I located the swimming pool.

The succession of levels, stepping down a hillside setting, recalled for me the villa gardens of France and Italy's Mediterranean coast. I decided to give this hill a similar treatment. Although borrowing an inspiration, I still didn't want to create a literal imitation of the European models. I decided to draw on the European tradition but in a way that would declare independence. I shaped the pool into a for-

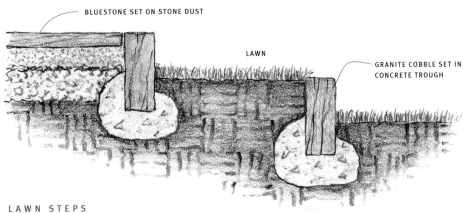

BLUESTONE SET ON STONE DUST

LAWN

GRANITE COBBLE SET IN CONCRETE TROUGH

LAWN STEPS

mal, aristocratic ellipse and connected it to the terrace above with a pair of curved paths—in the classic Old World style—but I set the paths off center, deliberately violating their symmetry. This was Versailles with a twist—a grand, formal gesture subverted (and softened) by this countryside's naturally curving hills and valleys.

Like the terrace, the pool enjoys sweeping views of the sound and the salt marsh that borders it. However, to retain a degree of intimacy, to keep it friendly, I framed the pool's wide steps with planting, which creates a kind of alcove where adults can sit and children can splash around. Surrounding the terrace I planted native grasses and perennial wildflowers that echo the wetland below.

This sequence of rooms is not the only axis of the garden. There's an intimate verandah on the other side of the house, which offers yet more views. Connecting to

another lawn terrace by a stepping stone path, it overlooks a woodland slope. There's also a large, paved, circular forecourt that is planted with flowering trees, evergreen shrubs, perennials, and grasses. Between this court and the front porch, I set a paved landing where the owners can receive guests and display their collection of planted urns and pots. Still another stone path leads to the less formal, family entrance, and this is planted as an English cottage garden.

Around all this graceful architecture I wove a relaxed network of

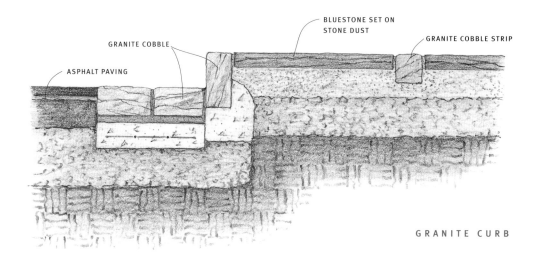

ASPHALT PAVING

GRANITE COBBLE

BLUESTONE SET ON STONE DUST

GRANITE COBBLE STRIP

GRANITE CURB

mulch paths, a web that meanders through surrounding woodland enriched with plantings of native ferns, ground covers, and shade-loving wildflowers. This is yet another contrast, in a garden of many. It was by the contrasts, though, and by the balancing of different elements that I managed to settle such a large house into its setting while still providing appropriately proportioned entrances and boundaries.

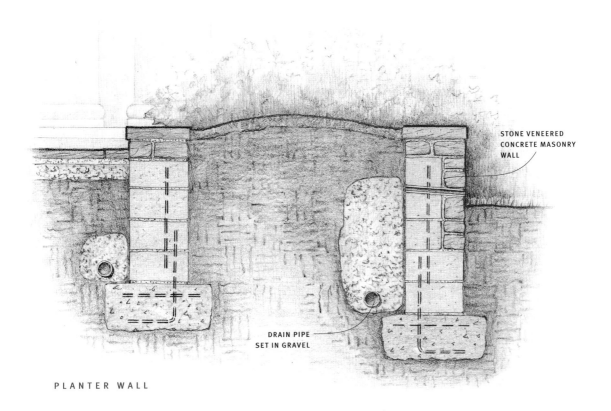

STONE VENEERED
CONCRETE MASONRY
WALL

DRAIN PIPE
SET IN GRAVEL

PLANTER WALL

INSPIRED BY STONE

chapter nine

I FIND STONE TO BE A POWERFULLY EVOCATIVE MATERIAL. IT

stirs up wonderful memories of mountains, cliffs, and waterfalls; of colored pebbles glistening at the

bottom of a stream; of crumbling walls and temples and the paths I've followed through venerable

gardens.

Humanity's first homes were stone caves, after all; the earliest boundaries dividing "ours" from

"theirs" were stone walls. All over the world, the history of countries is mapped in the paths, fortifica-

tions, benches, and walls that people fashioned from stone.

Stone has a special power in a garden setting. Because it comes out of the earth, stone even

when cut and shaped still links us to the natural world much as plants do. Indeed, it's the natural com-

plement to plants, an obvious material for garden making. Moreover, whereas man-made materials

commonly grow shabby as they age, stone improves with the passage of time. It's like wood in that

respect: stone weathers handsomely. As rain, wind, and frost soften the corners and lichen creeps

across its surface, stone takes on a dignity and authority.

When I'm building in stone, I feel that I'm building for the ages. In choosing the type of stone best suited to the site, I let the garden's location advise me. On occasion, the setting may tell me that no stone at all is a good choice. At the edge of a sandy beach, for example, a fieldstone wall is likely to seem at odds with the site. There wood or even concrete would seem more appropriate to me. However, on a mountainside or a rocky meadow, anywhere that stone is part of the natural scene, I feel free to use it in my architecture.

There are other considerations in selecting the type of stone best suited to a particular garden, of course. In a garden adjoining a stone house, I like to use the same or a similar type of stone in my construction, to help pull the house out into the garden. Commonly, I'll use the matching stone to build the walls that run out from the house and then build the terraces, steps, and paths out of some contrasting material, such as brick or concrete. In general, the stone I select for the vertical plane—for walls, for example—I avoid using on the horizontal plane, such as pavements.

Different kinds of stone create different impressions. For a city garden, I'd be likely to select a smooth limestone or granite paving; for a country garden, I might opt for rugged fieldstone slabs. In addition, your choice of stone should also reflect the function you want the material to perform. Some kinds of stone work well for paving, others for garden sculpture or containers, and still others for coping around pools and ponds. When I feel the site can handle it, I may mix several kinds of stone to enrich the garden's overall design.

I recommend that clients build in stone whenever possible. Its initial cost is high, but because stone lasts so well in the garden, over the years it usually works out to be a bargain. Though durable, stone is not maintenance free. In particular, if they have been laid with mortar, stones will need repointing periodically. In general, though, stone requires the least maintenance of any architectural material.

- GRANITE. A hard-wearing, ruggedly handsome stone, granite is wonderful for paving. Its durability also makes it ideal for driveways, street curbs, and sculptures that are exposed to the elements. It's also an excellent stone for fountains. When polished, granite varies in color from pink and white to gray and black. It makes an attractive, long-lasting veneer for walls.

- LIMESTONE. Limestone is porous and softer both in appearance and in fact than granite. Not as enduring, limestone can weather rapidly if exposed to acid rain. Nevertheless, it makes a very attractive material for paving, wall veneers, stepping stones, and fountains. Its warm, off-white color combines well with brick.

- PENNSYLVANIA BLUESTONE. An East Coast native, Pennsylvania bluestone is a sedimentary rock, which means that it is deposited in layers; its tendency, therefore, is to split into wide, flat sheets. This makes it excellent for use in paving or for a coping to edge a swimming pool. Though relatively hard, bluestone is easy to cut and easily worked into patterned designs for elegant terraces. Because it splits relatively easily along a horizontal plane, bluestone is unsuitable as a material for sculpture.

- **SLATE AND BASALT.** I don't often use either slate or basalt in paving because they both are slippery when wet, and their dark colors cause them to absorb sunlight easily and become uncomfortably hot in summertime. Still, the combination of swarthy hues and smooth textures of slates and basalts can be very beautiful.

- **SANDSTONE.** Sandstone is another porous rock that works well as a material for wall copings, steps, sculpture, and paving and also for planters. The sandstones commonly found in stoneyards range in color from light gray to a creamy pink.

- **MARBLE.** Marble is the ultimate stone for sculpture or for garden benches, but because it wears easily, anything made from it should be set in a protected spot, such as a niche in a wall, where it won't be subjected to the full effects of the weather or to salt spray. Marble is not a suitable material for paving, because of its fine texture: it becomes very slippery when wet.

- **FIELDSTONE.** Fieldstone is a label that stone yards apply to a wide variety of different kinds of stone, which is gathered from the surface of the ground rather than being extracted from a quarry. Fieldstone, which is furnished uncut, with the natural, irregular surfaces, lends a rustic, informal look to anything built from it. When buying fieldstone, I often choose Stonyhurst flagging or Roxbury granite. Alternatively, I may use whatever fieldstone I find on the site. In any case, I prefer a fieldstone with an earthy natural color, such as brown or beige.

One of my special enthusiasms when designing gardens is for low walls in which the stone has been laid "dry"; that is, without mortar. In such a drystone wall, the individual stones are held in place only by friction and gravity. This may sound precarious, but in fact a well-laid drystone wall can be extremely durable. The seasonal heave of the frost presents no danger to a structure whose stones can ride up and then settle back with the thaw. Movement of this sort would shatter a mortared wall. Aside from the durability of drystone walls, I also prize the way they integrate with the landscape. Small plants root into the crevices between rocks, and as the stone weathers, the individual stones merge visually to create an overall texture. In a couple of years your wall will begin to look as if it had always been there, a natural outgrowth of the earth. I'll often enhance this natural appearance by deliberately leaving hollows in the top of some sections of a dry wall and planting them myself. Similarly, I like to set in herbs, mosses, or small flowering plants between the stones of a pathway (page 182) or into crevices of a terraced area where traffic is light.

Although I like drystone construction, a mortared wall also has its virtues and advantages. It has a more finished, architectural look and is more at home in an elegant or formal design. The stone used for such mortared work can be sharp and pristine, or it can be rugged in its natural texture and relief. A mortared wall also expresses strength and longevity, but because it cannot shift without shattering it must be set on a footing, a stable foundation that extends down into the earth below the depth to which the frost penetrates in your region. This increases the cost of the mortared wall, but is essential to ensure the permanence and accuracy of your design.

In addition to such obviously man-made structures, you may wish to use stone to create seemingly natural features. If your property offers a gentle slope, for example, you may wish to construct a rock garden. To do that, I build up the soil with coarse sand and sphagnum peat first. Then I set the stones into the slope so that just the upper part of each is exposed. Into the gaps and crevices between the stones I set alpine plants and dwarf trees and shrubs to create a sort of geological garden sculpture.

There is another sort of naturalistic feature that I incorporate into many of my garden designs, and that is a variation on the traditional Japanese dry streambed. The Japanese create channels lined with rounded, water-polished stones to create the impression of a waterway. I will meander a stone path down a slope to achieve the same effect and to link in a harmonious manner terraces, walls, and rock gardens. Boulders carefully situated along a slope not only furnish convenient stepping stones but also fool the eye into thinking that there is a brook racing down the slope just out of sight—all that is missing is the sound of rushing water. Such a "stream" can terminate in a stone terrace, to suggest a plunge into a mountain pool, and all without the spilling of a single drop of real moisture.

My advice about working on a generous rather than a stingy scale is especially important when working with stone. Don't be timid; let loose. Think of yourself as a sculptor. Then cover your stone surfaces, paths, and walks with plants that will soften their edges, cool their hot surfaces, and create a luxuriant contrast to the adamantine surface of the rock. When you've finished digging in the last plant, put down your trowel and sit back. You'll enjoy the satisfaction of knowing that what you have created will give pleasure for many years.

THE DIAMOND

GARDEN

PEOPLE ARE COMPLEX. WE ALL HAVE MORE than one side, and our gardens, if they are truly to fit us, must be multifaceted too. That's why my exposition of the gardens in this book has been a bit simplistic. Each garden has been made to illustrate a single principle, yet all could easily fit into several different categories. The Nef garden (page 81), for example, I used as an example of the integration of works of art into the garden. However, it could just as easily have served as an illustration of the architecture of the small town garden. Similarly, the garden I share with you in the next few pages, the Diamond garden, does provide an outstanding lesson in the role stone can play in garden architecture. It's also a fine demonstration of the importance of working with a site's topography and of how to use water and (once again) art to further a design. The fact that this large country garden includes not a single scrap of lawn also sets it apart.

These 36 acres of moody semiwilderness in Westchester County, New York, is

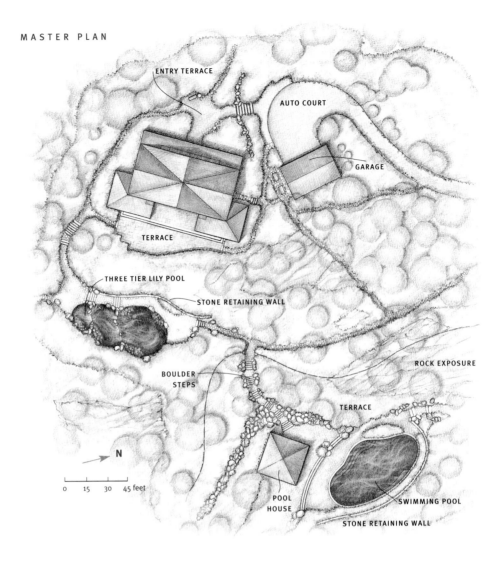

ENTRY TERRACE

AUTO COURT

GARAGE

TERRACE

THREE TIER LILY POOL

STONE RETAINING WALL

BOULDER
STEPS

ROCK EXPOSURE

TERRACE

N

0   15   30   45 feet

POOL
HOUSE

SWIMMING POOL

STONE RETAINING WALL

indeed a place apart. New York City is less than an hour's drive away, but this land

belongs to another, very different world. Its wild and rocky terrain reminds me of

paintings by artists of the Hudson River school. Fortunately, the present owners

of the property, Janice and Robert Diamond, appreciate its distinctive character and

have been careful to respect it even while domesticating it. The many mature trees on

the site were carefully preserved, and the shingled house and guest cottage the

Diamonds built were cleverly nestled into the outcroppings. Rather than attacking

the rocky ribs of the landscape, the Diamonds allowed me to capitalize on them. As a result, I was able to create here what amounted to a spacious rock garden, but a rock garden of a most unconventional sort—a rhapsody in stone.

Unlike many gardens I've created for a large landscape, the Diamond garden is not designed on an axis. Instead, it flows downward from the house, from plateau to plateau, around and through stands of trees, meadows, and rocky overlooks. Paths and massive steps of rustic stone bind together the various parts, linking dwellings and pool, leading the visitor up and down and through the sweeps of perennials and shrubs.

The plan appears unstructured—it seems just an accident of the local geology—and yet considerable art was devoted to making the garden follow the natural curves of the landscapes. Clean-edged borders or rugs of patterned stone, the devices I customarily use to define spaces, would not fit here. In their place, I used boulders, granite stairs, and rocky paths to create an archaic "floor" that respects the site's topography. Denied the use of right angles and clearly drawn formal boundaries, I used works from the Diamonds' collection of contemporary sculpture to contain the spaces, placing them strategically to catch, hold, and direct the eye.

Water, a natural counterpoint to stone, is a central element of this garden. Dropping down from the house, you wander along a series of cascading pools and a three-tiered lily pond, arriving finally at the swimming pool. This last I designed to serve an aesthetic as well as recreational func- tion. The pool is the place for a sum-

mertime swim, of course, but it is also set so as to mirror the spectacular rock bluff that overlooks it. When the afternoon sun angles in to strike the terrace, lighting the countless flecks of mica in the stone, this whole area gleams silver, merging into the clouds of gray-leaved herbs with which it is framed.

In this garden you can spend an afternoon admiring the music of water over stone and the cries of hawks. You can take a solitary walk along woodland paths. You can lounge in the sun in the warm weather; in fall and winter you can admire the plump Fernando Botero nude sunbathing on the marble plinth that floats above the bed of fawn-colored grasses. In any season, with its generous, flowing atmosphere of a wilderness park, this garden shows the wisdom of occasionally letting the straight edge of the designer's T-square gather some dust.

Fernando Botero, *Nude Lying on Her Stomach Smoking a Cigarette*. Bronze.

I chose to include it here for another reason, however. I've already shown many examples of how to use stone to shore up untidy edges in a garden, to create boundaries and outdoor "rugs," and to imply a mood of permanence and strength. This garden tells a different version of that story. The dramatic, almost mythic, landscape demonstrates how stone that occurs naturally in a garden can influence an entire design, create a mood, or set the stage.

PART THREE

GALLERY OF ARCHITECTURAL FEATURES

ARCHITECTURAL DETAILS OUGHT NEVER TO
DOMINATE THE GARDEN, BUT ALWAYS TO
ENHANCE THE TEXTURES AND FEATURES OF NATURE.

—Rosemary Verey

Paths, Terraces, and Driveways

PAVED SURFACES DEFINE A GARDEN'S BASIC structure and organization. They are a major element of the garden, the basic structure around which secondary elements arrange themselves. The paved areas are the hardest-working parts of the garden; by defining the areas of use, they also set the framework for the planting. Because of their importance, I typically design paved surfaces first.

The paving plans for your garden should be based on a few principles. To begin with, keep in mind that these are, fundamentally, utilitarian features. Each paved surface should be designed for a specific purpose or purposes. Paths and walkways,

for example, should be laid out so as to lead visitors comfortably, safely, and as conveniently as possible from place to place. That may seem obvious, but think how often you've seen a dirt track cut though a lawn because the hard-surfaced path that was supposed to accommodate foot traffic pursued an unnecessarily indirect or otherwise inconvenient route.

Like paths, terraces should be designed to accommodate intended activities. Thus, a terrace

and pattern affect our perception of its scale. Finer textures make tight spaces appear larger. For example, try turning brick or paving stones on edge rather than laying them flat. In small spaces this finer texture creates an illusion of greater expanse. This sort of treatment will force you to use more of the pavers to surface the same area, but you may decide that the effect is worth the extra expense.

A terrace always looks larger on a drawing than it does when actually laid out in the garden. That's why, when designing a terrace, I always err

intended for nighttime entertaining should be smoothly (but not slickly) paved to prevent accidents in low-light conditions. It should also be appropriately lit and placed conveniently to the house. Likewise, driveways should provide convenient access and parking for cars.

Choose pavement materials, colors, and textures that you can live with. Tile, brick, or precisely cut stone laid in predictable patterns with crisp, well-defined edges give a paved area a more finished look, whereas randomly placed flagstone or loosely set brick produce a much more casual appearance.

Remember that a paving material's texture

sure to friends' gardens and see how much space is required by each of the elements you want to include. Don't obsess about what will go where, though. The exact layout is not as critical at this point as the total space required.

There are a few practical aspects to consider too when choosing a paving material. For example, light-colored pavements—those made of concrete with exposed aggregate, for example—are reflective and so tend to be cooler underfoot on hot, sunny days. Hard and uneven surfaces are less comfortable for activities such as dancing or standing for long periods of time. Smooth tile finishes can be hazardous because they become slippery when wet.

on the side of big. However, designing a terrace to the proper size is more than just guesswork. I try to base my dimensions on hard data. Think about how much entertaining you will do and how much space will be required for such accessories as furniture, umbrellas, and barbecue grills. Take a tape mea-

PAVING WITH STONE. Stone is the classic material for paving and remains one of the best. Many different kinds are suitable for this use: limestone,

bluestone, granite cobbles, and various types of flagstone are just a few. Your choice will be dictated in part by the use for which your pavement is intended—cobblestones, for example, would make a poor surface for an open-air dance floor—but also by what harmonizes aesthetically with the rest of the garden. Stone of local origin usually fits most naturally into any landscape and is often the cheapest item at the local stoneyard. In addition to

price, however, you should consider color, surface textures, local availability, and cold weather (porous materials that absorb water are not suitable in colder climates).

How you set the stone will also affect its look, and indeed the look of the whole garden. Stones set in a random pattern and without a regular perimeter give a pavement a very informal air, and I like to enhance this by encouraging creeping plants to colonize the gaps between the

stones. You create a dressier look by placing stones within regular, neatly defined borders and by reducing the width of the joints between

BRICK. Brick is a versatile paving material that is made in many colors and textures. It can be laid in patterns, either set flat for simplicity and economy or set on edge to enhance its textural interest. In an informal landscape you may choose to lay the bricks without mortar on a simple bed of sand; for a more finished look you should first lay down a rigid base of concrete or asphalt, set the bricks on that, and fill the joints with mortar. I often use "stringers"—bands of some contrasting material such as limestone—to relieve the monotony of large areas of pavement. With brick surfaces, one of my favorite techniques is to inlay a pattern of stone stringers to create a decorative quilt effect.

stones. Cut stone laid in geometric courses on a rigid base is even more formal in effect.

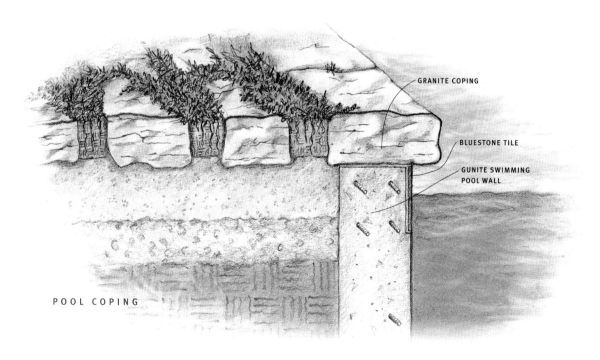

GRANITE COPING

BLUESTONE TILE

GUNITE SWIMMING
POOL WALL

POOL COPING

ment with little work. Because of concrete's relatively low cost and ease of maintenance it is a popular material for driveways and parking courts.

TILE. Tile is a material that combines the convenience of a molded, man-made material with an attractively natural, earthy look. Tiles come in many colors, shapes, and textures. For large expanses of pavement, I favor those with subdued colors. However, I'll often combine them with an inset of livelier tiles, those with flashy colors and intricate shapes that can draw attention to selected garden features.

Some tiles, particularly those like the terra-

CONCRETE. Concrete, though often disparaged, is actually quite a versatile as well as economical material. When newly poured, it can be formed into almost any shape and finished in many patterns and textures. Concrete's natural color is drab, but it can easily be enlivened by tinting it with various pigments while it is being mixed. Concrete can also be given a pleasant, pebbly texture by washing it after it has been poured and while it is still curing to expose the "aggregate," the gravel that is one element of the mix.

You'll also find precast concrete pavers at home supply centers, and many of these are designed to lock together to provide a very tight, durable pave-

cotta tiles, which are fired at lower temperatures, do not stand up well in cold northern winters. Glazed tiles are also unsuitable for high-traffic areas outdoors because their slippery surface can easily become dangerously slick when wet. Another limitation of tiles is that as a paving material they require a rigid base with a clean, well-defined edge.

OTHER MATERIALS. We ordinarily think of garden paving in terms of hard materials only, but soft-surfaced materials may be made to serve a similar purpose. I often use turf, mulch, and gravel in much the same way as pavement in my designs, using them all like rugs in an outdoor room.

Finally, when designing and installing pavements, keep in mind that terraces invite adornment. Their edges provide an irresistible foil for plantings. Balustrades, overlook platforms, bold retaining walls, intriguing steps and ramps that lead from one level to the next, and even the overspill of a waterfall can, along with other works of fancy, make your garden terrace sparkle.

Bridges, Boardwalks, and Decks

ELEVATED GARDEN STRUCTURES NOT ONLY LEAD us from place to place but also allow us to experience the garden from a new perspective. Besides

enhancing access from one part of the garden to another, structures of this kind stand as reminders of journeys taken and encouragement for trips yet to be made. For this reason, footbridges, board-

walks, and elevated decks are a rich source of drama and, with their promise of a voyage to the unknown, of mystery as well.

Footbridges allow us to be as close as possible to the water in our garden. If you are fortunate

Suitable bridge materials include various combinations of wood, stone, concrete, and steel. A bridge can be suspended from above, supported from the ground on posts, or simply stretched on

enough to have a pond or stream, consider enhancing its allure by adding a bridge.

Your footbridge can be straight, curved, offset, or zigzagged, and it can have a rustic, classical, or contemporary look. You may choose to keep it as close to the water's surface as possible or arched above it for a better view.

stringers across small crossings. To bridge a shallow channel, you might consider simply laying a sequence of stepping stones.

tions of the structure. Likewise, you can further elaborate it with embellishments such as built-in seating and decorative balustrades to give the bridge special character.

Boardwalks also provide a "bridge" to garden places that otherwise may not be accessible—marshy areas or steep and slippery slopes, for example. In addition to these practical functions, boardwalks also serve as a sort of visual punctuation, providing a strong, bold line that separates the garden into zones while at the same time linking the house with major garden features such as ponds, rock outcroppings, and specimen plants.

At its simplest, a boardwalk is just a pathway, but you can also treat it as a staging area for special experiences. For example, widen your boardwalk under the overhanging branches of a shade tree and add benches. Make that stretch of boardwalk a retreat for those in need of quiet. Add steps or turnouts near special views. Extend

Keep in mind when you are designing your bridge that it can be more than a simple footpath. You may choose to roof or partially enclose por-

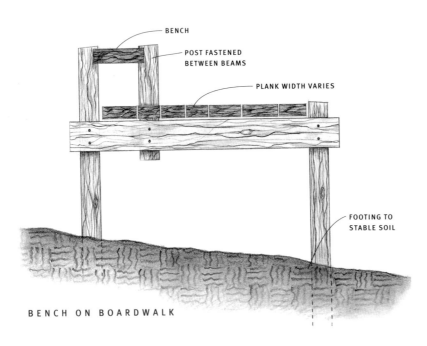

BENCH

POST FASTENED BETWEEN BEAMS

PLANK WIDTH VARIES

FOOTING TO STABLE SOIL

BENCH ON BOARDWALK

provide beautiful garden views. Easy to install and adaptable, decks are especially practical features on steeply sloping sites where creating a conventional, ground-level terrace is out of the question.

Whether a deck is attached to the house or placed freestanding in the middle of the garden, this man-made space is an irresistible place to

the boardwalk around a pond to a gazebo where guests can enjoy afternoon tea at waterside. In addition, make a point of playing up the relationship between plants and the boardwalk. When I am designing such a structure, I like to set it into the landscape so that it seems almost to disappear into the overhanging plants that spring upward in summer.

A deck is a different, more self-contained type of elevated structure. Instead of providing a passage from here to there, it is an end in itself, an artificial plateau that can expand the living space of your home and

dine, entertain, or pass the time of day. Because of its elevation above ground level, a deck can also furnish a superb vantage point for enjoying an over-

view of the garden or for gathering in the "borrowed scenery" of distant views. Outdoor furniture and fixtures enhance a deck's "garden room" ambience, and the eye-level perspective into foliage of nearby trees that a deck can offer is an added visual treat.

Think of your deck as a part of the garden, not as part of the house, and follow some basic rules for design. Select materials and colors that are in keeping with other garden improvements and house details. Be sure that the plants you set into containers on the deck complement the surrounding ground-level planting. Leave openings in the deck for new plants, or let existing trees penetrate it from below (leaving plenty of space for trunks to expand and sway in the breeze). If access to or from your deck requires a long stairway, divide this into a number of flights and landings that step up or down a slope in a gradual and natural way.

Edges

IN THE SENSE THAT AN EDGE IS THE line along which something begins or ends, gardens are full of edges. As a garden designer, my job is largely an exercise in manipulating edges. If you look carefully at any of the gardens illustrated in this book, you will see just how important edges are.

Since edges are drawn wherever contrasting materials meet, almost anything you do in the garden results in an edge. If you build a fence, lay a terrace, dig a pool, or erect a retaining wall, you create edges. Nature draws powerful edges also. Streams, lakeshores, marsh boundaries, rock outcroppings, and shadow lines are just a few examples of the natural features that define edges; these are the lines that anchor our garden designs.

Although some edges are as simple as the curb line that defines your garden path, I want you to think of them in a much broader context and use them to support your design theme.

First, learn to distinguish between "hard" and "soft" edges. Hard edges occur where contrasting materials bump into each other—where a brick terrace meets a lawn, for example. Soft edges are subtler. They commonly occur where planting or a change in elevation masks the exact line of transition.

The difference between a hard and soft edge is more than just a matter of precision. The two types of edge create different impressions on the

viewer and so are suited to different styles of design. The crisp line of a hard edge lends itself to the geometry and symmetry of a formal design, whereas the relaxed shapes and sweeping lines common to soft edges promote a more casual, informal garden style.

Look again at some of your favorite gardens to learn how the treatment of edges has influenced their overall design. Notice how the hard edges of a paved driveway, for example, define spaces next to them that can be used as garden features— perhaps as a planted forecourt. Notice how the designer or gardener may have softened a hard

Whether the edges you design are soft and free-flowing or more geometric in character, they must be deliberate. They must exist for a reason. In other words, you must pay close attention to the

edge by overlaying it with a ground cover or cascading plants. Be aware of subtle edges too, such as the one that occurs when a lawn fades into a surrounding wood.

garden spaces that your edges define. Make sure the edges you create yield spaces that are pleasing to the eye and have a functional or visual meaning. An edge might work to contain a plant mass, like a belt around a waist. Alternatively, the edge itself

might serve for some activity, as in the case of a paved path, or it might mark the transition to a particular activity, as in the edges that enclose a play court or dining terrace. Often an edge is included purely to give pleasure, as in the neat, manicured edge of a lawn, which makes such a satisfying foil to the dramatic planting beyond.

All in all, be sure to lay out your edges carefully. They give your garden its sense of order and expansiveness.

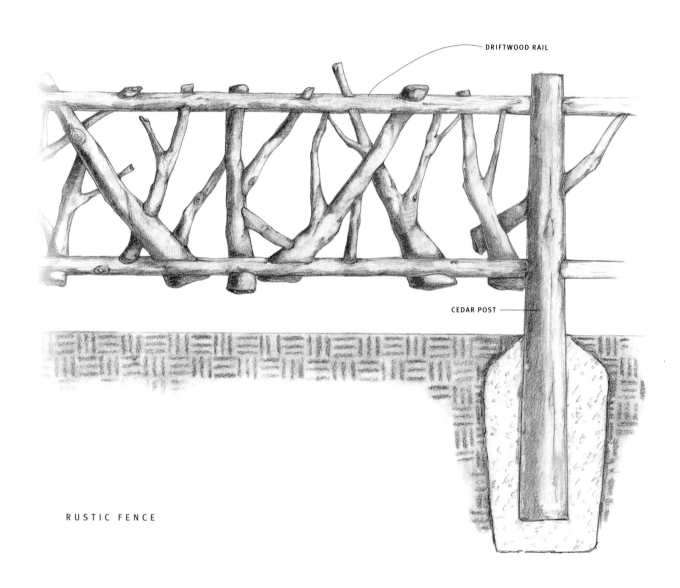

DRIFTWOOD RAIL

CEDAR POST

RUSTIC FENCE

design process is to select the style and the material that suits your needs and preferences. When I'm designing a fence, I look for materials that are in keeping with the garden's character. If the garden is soft and informal, preservative-treated or naturally rot-resistant wood (such as cedar) may be

appropriate. Wood weathers nicely, and it's okay to let it disappear under mounds of perennials during the summer. If the garden is more formal, consider an ornamental or classical design, perhaps using wrought iron or painted wooden pickets. Remember that posts can be enhanced with playful caps or finials that match the details and colors of your house and extend its character into the garden.

If you live in the country, you may not want to

interrupt your view with a fence. If your site offers a suitable slope, you can create an equally effective but virtually invisible barrier by installing a ha-ha  (see page 207). A ha-ha is a barrier set into a cut in the side of a slope; the goal is to depress the barrier below the line of sight. In a rural setting a ha-ha can create the impression that the horses or sheep in the neighboring field can wander right up to the house, but in fact their access is securely barred.

As with any other kind of architectural feature, a well-designed fence does not exist in isolation. It should always be designed to work in context with other garden improvements, such as benches, tables and chairs, lighting fixtures, plant containers, arbors, paved areas, and walls. The fence must work practically and aesthetically with the other built elements.

Stairs and Steps

CHANGES IN ELEVATION ARE A GREAT resource to a garden, and if you are so fortunate as to have a sloping site be sure to make the most of it. This will mean giving full consideration to stairs and steps, as well as to ramps and inclined paths. These architectural elements are the means by which a gardener extracts the benefits from topography.

What, specifically, are the benefits of steps and stairs? They can lead you to special garden places and unexpected views. They can also be decorative and playful. They infuse a garden with surprise, as, for example, when we change direction at a landing. When we work our way blindly up a steep slope by a series of switchbacks, the steps and stairs become a source of mystery. They can create an aura of peacefulness, as when we ascend a stone path that reminds us of a dry streambed. Stairs are also useful for choreographing the visitor's view: if properly arranged, they can serve as a progression of viewing platforms that draw attention either to distant scenery or to close-up garden features and plant displays. Practically speaking,

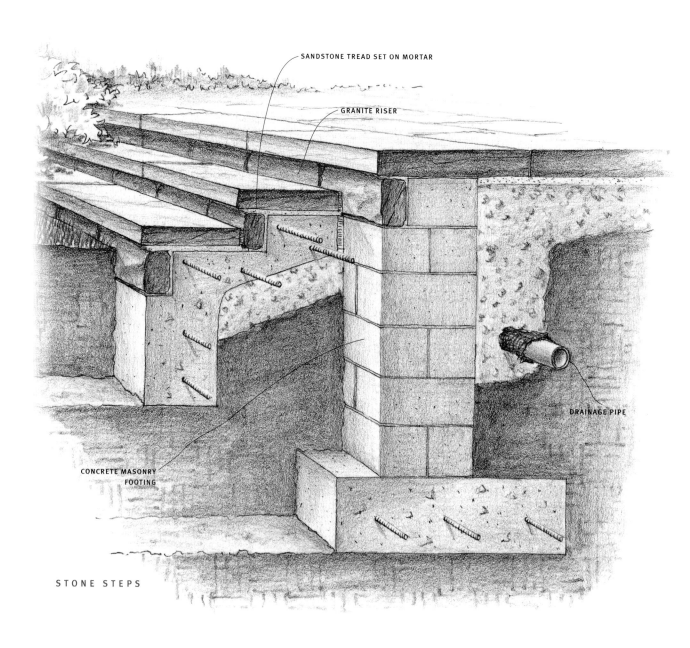

SANDSTONE TREAD SET ON MORTAR

GRANITE RISER

DRAINAGE PIPE

CONCRETE MASONRY
FOOTING

STONE STEPS

stairs and steps are essential organizational devices. By marking the transition from one level of the landscape to another, they not only connect but also define the different areas, distinguishing and linking pool with dining terrace and deck, for example.

You will need to follow simple guidelines to ensure easy movement from one level to another in

tioned. The riser (the vertical dimension of the step) can vary from about 4 to about 6 inches, and the tread (the front to back horizontal dimension) from about 12 to about 18 inches. A simple rule to remember about this relationship is that shorter risers require wider treads. For example, a combi-

the garden. A ramp or inclined path is suitable for modest grade changes (up to 10 percent or 12 percent), but steps are needed for steeper slopes. Occasional landings may be needed to break up longer runs of steps; placing them where special garden features and views occur is a bonus.

Step risers and treads should be uniformly spaced and carefully propor-

nation 4-inch riser and 18-inch tread is acceptable, but a 6-inch riser should have a tread of 14 inches or less. Such variations of riser and tread are necessary to fit the steps to the slope. A low, long slope requires a longer tread; a steep slope dictates a loftier riser. The object, however, is always the same: to allow the person using the stairs to complete a full, comfortable stride in moving from step to step. The only exception to this rule comes when the slope is very long and low, so that the width of each tread may stretch to 18 inches or more. In that case, the user will need more than one stride to cross the

tread, and you must calculate the tread and riser relationship to fit not a single stride but a multiple one. In any case, though, the length of an average stride remains the basic unit of measurement when designing steps.

Once again, there are many materials from which to choose when building steps and stairs. Your selection should enhance the style of the garden as a whole. Cut stone, brick laid in mortar on a rigid base, and carefully finished concrete generally create an impression of formality. Steps created by overlapping fieldstones, or by a framing of wood timbers infilled with brick laid on sand have a more casual look. Handrails, balustrades, and other fenestration details should complement your

design. Above all, when designing the steps for your garden, remember that the object should be not only utility but also the enhancement of the house and garden as a whole. Study the architectural details of your house and accompanying arbors or bridge railings before

selecting materials and drawing up plans so that

the steps you create will not only take you where

you want to go but will also become the essential

link that unifies house and grounds.

Walls

ERECTING A WALL IS A BIG EXPENSE, but it can also have a big impact on a garden. What's more, this impact can be aesthetic as well as functional. Well-designed garden walls give privacy, security, and protection against wind. They also provide an especially satisfying means for marking the garden's outer boundaries or for defining areas intended for special activities or special sorts of plantings. Walls are the most convincing devices for marking garden rooms and are ideal surfaces for the display of fountains, sculpture, and artworks. They work equally well as the backdrop and support for trellises and climbing plants. In short, regardless of your garden's size or shape, there's an opportunity

there for a wall, and walls that are properly placed, dimensioned, and detailed will add immeasurably to your garden's charm and overall sense of organization.

Begin to plan for your walls by thinking about what kind of outdoor "room" you'd like to have. A simple garden wall can define an intimate outdoor living space by creating a secluded exten-

Don't get locked into linear thinking. Remember that walls don't have to follow a straight line; they can have graceful curves, turn corners, or be arranged in an offset fashion. Likewise, be resourceful. Use what's already there. A garage wall can also serve as a garden wall, or maybe you can "borrow" the back of the wall that a neighbor has erected to mark the edge of his or her property.

sion to a kitchen or dining area, for example. Think also about how your wall could carry the architecture of your house into the garden and thus integrate the indoor and outdoor parts of your living environment.

Take advantage of the outer edge of a raised planting bed. That can become a garden wall, as can the pool enclosure.

One note of caution: If you are fortunate enough to have an expansive vista of "borrowed

security and order. Soils adjacent to the top of a retaining wall form a perfect platform for planting. Cascading plants not only soften the appearance of such a

scenery," make sure your walls don't compromise it.

A special kind of garden wall, one that is often a necessity on a steeply sloping site, is the retaining wall. Even where the slope is more moderate, a retaining wall can, by leveling the area above and below, make the garden much more accessible, usable, and pleasing to the eye.

Use retaining walls to define progressive garden layers, carve out a pool terrace, or support comfortable garden benches. Properly placed, they endow the garden with a sense of

wall but also keep visitors safely away from the edge. Similarly, in rural settings you may want to consider a ha-ha (see page 208).

Where steep slopes are involved, it usually is preferable to install a series of retaining walls of lesser height rather than just one or two lofty ones. The lower walls are inherently sturdier and better able to resist the outward pressure of the earth they are designed to hold back. Higher walls tend to look forbidding. They are also more difficult to negotiate (requiring longer flights of stairs or ramps) and more likely to interrupt views.

The best materials for a wall include stone, brick, rot-resistant timber, and concrete (either in preformed blocks or cast in place). The material you select should complement those used in your house and elsewhere in the garden. But you can also adapt a mate-

rial to the needs and style of your house and garden by the way you use it. Stone, for example, can be given a formal look by laying it in a precise pattern.

Simply stacked in a random pattern like natural outcroppings, it produces a wall with a far more relaxed look.

Good craftsmanship and good advice are key to safety when it comes to garden walls. Even a wall of modest height will incorporate a huge weight of materials, and if it topples severe injury may result. While designing your wall, be sure to consult with a qualified engineer or other design professional regarding dimensions, safety features, and structural details. Their help will also ensure that your wall meets the specifications required by local government agencies and will qualify for any necessary permits.

RAISED POOL WALL AND FOUNTAIN

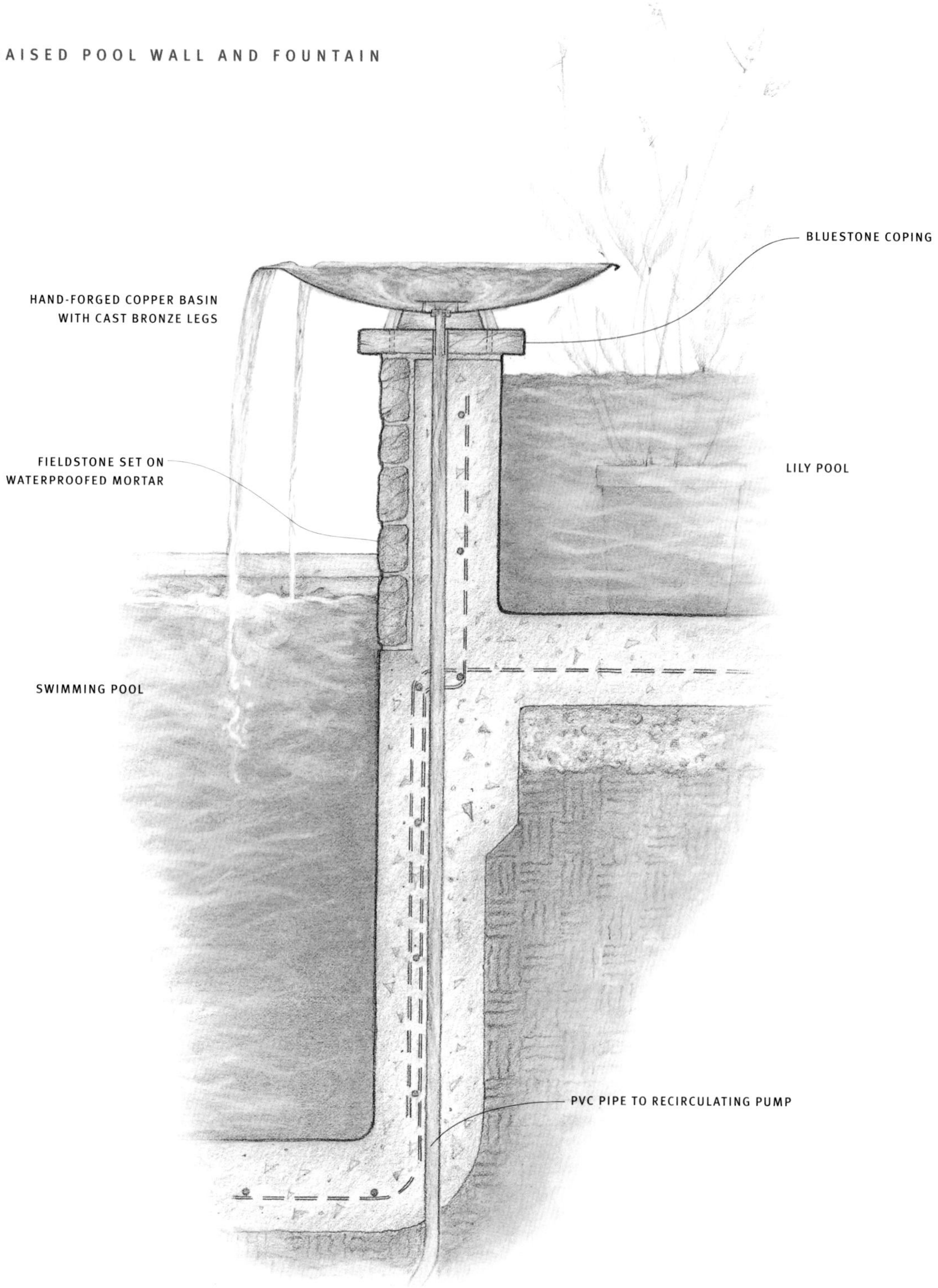

BLUESTONE COPING

HAND-FORGED COPPER BASIN
WITH CAST BRONZE LEGS

LILY POOL

FIELDSTONE SET ON
WATERPROOFED MORTAR

SWIMMING POOL

PVC PIPE TO RECIRCULATING PUMP

Waterworks

EARLY GARDENERS NEEDED A pool or fountain from which they could draw buckets of water to irrigate their plantings. Today such waterworks continue to play a major role in the garden because of the unique pleasures they can provide to the gardeners and their guests. I use many kinds of water features in my designs—courtyard wall fountains, lily pools, swimming pools, ponds, and recirculating fountains and waterfalls. Even the illusion of water can sometimes be enough: I've also built "dry streams," channels filled with rounded river rocks, to create the impression that a gush of water is imminent. Wherever possible I also take advantage of natural water sources, playing up the views of a bay, river, or pond that can add beauty and mystery to the garden.

Water in any quantity can transform a garden. The reflections in a tiny dish of rainwater brighten a town house courtyard, and a river's broad surface will extend a garden's reach far beyond its legal boundaries. Waterworks can accentuate the expansive qualities of a horizontal site in

this way, just as water tumbling can turn the retaining walls of a sloping site into a lively cascade.

Even though irrigation comes now with a twist of the tap, waterworks still offer practical as well as aesthetic benefits to the gardener. A pool can be a welcome source of recreation, of course, or a home for waterfowl and lush aquatic plants. A fountain's spray cools the surrounding area on hot days, and it serves as a generator of white noise that masks unpleasant background racket, helping to insulate the garden from the outer world.

I wrote extensively about designing water features in the first book of this series, *Gardening with Water,* but the following points bear mentioning here:

- Make your pool or pond as large as possible within its dedicated space. Pools look much larger on the drawing board than they do on the site. Don't skimp.

- If you have a large site, let the water relate to its immediate surroundings. For example, a pond that is remote from the house and adjacent to a woods or pasture should be free-form and natural looking, but if it's close to the house or another outdoor structure such as a deck it should be geo-

metric in shape and more finished in appearance.

• Curved lines make small spaces look smaller; stick with symmetrical shapes—squares and rectangles—if your garden is small.

• Don't overlook important legal and practical restrictions that may apply

when designing your water features. Most jurisdictions have rigid codes that regulate placement, setbacks, depth, protective fencing, drainage, the availability of necessary utilities, and other safety and operational matters.

- Don't forget that excavating and installing a water feature is likely to require heavy construction equipment, so your garden design must allow them access to the site.

Lighting

WITHOUT A DOUBT, THE MOON AND stars are the most poetic illumination for your garden, but they aren't the most artful, or the most practical, especially on an overcast night. The lighting you provide is more reliable. It's also one of your most effective design tools. You can wield it like a paintbrush to paint nocturnal views of your garden, both from inside and outside the house. The lighting can enhance or shatter a garden's mystery, and as the garden changes with the seasons so should its lighting.

During the preparation of this book, I discussed the use of light in the garden with independent lighting designer Debra Gilmore. She shared ideas with me about various types of garden lights, which I now share with you.

HOUSE LIGHTS. Treat your house as a lantern that glows in any season or weather. The glow that emerges from your house at night should be included as an element in any lighting design you develop for your garden. Consider which lights you should leave burning at night to enhance the desired effect.

The lighting fixtures that best serve these purposes will differ from the ones you'll use for outdoor entertaining. The fixtures you'll install for that purpose should be calculated to create a festive or romantic atmosphere. Of course, the lighting you'll want to provide for a pool party of exuberant teenagers will be different from what you wish to furnish for a quiet cocktail party on the terrace overlooking the pond.

Finally, you should plan the lighting so that

TASK LIGHTS. Garden illumination serves a number of purposes and each of the tasks requires the appropriate kind of light. Any good lighting supply store can advise you on the best fixtures for a specific use. Before you go shopping, however, you should develop a clear plan of the kinds of effects you want to create.

Your first consideration in developing a lighting design is most likely to be security and safety. Most basically, you'll need lights to guide you into the house when you arrive home after sunset and lights that will deter unwanted visitors.

it makes possible the safe enjoyment of a nighttime stroll in the garden. Paths can be defined through a series of understated light fixtures, or you can delineate the path with lighting that's hidden within elements such as pavers, stairs, trees, arbors, or trellises.

You'll want to consider all your potential evening or nighttime activities when you are designing a lighting plan. Because experience may not match expectation, though, and because needs and interests can change, you should also make sure that any scheme you develop is flexible.

AMBIENT LIGHTS. A well-designed garden should offer a balanced and rich composition of light, which, in addition to task lighting, will almost surely include ambient light that washes walls and paving. There are several of kinds of mini-architectural floodlight fixtures that can provide such ambient light: mushroom floods with dimmers can be used for this purpose, or you may rely on a well-placed post top or pole-mounted fixture. How much ambient light you'll want to provide will depend partly on the location. In a city garden you

may derive much of what you want from the light that spills in from streetlights or from the lights in neighbors' houses or apartments.

ACCENT LIGHTS. Use accent light to increase the contrast between the ambient light and the task light in your garden. For example, you may use an accent light to illuminate a piece of sculpture or a specimen plant and reveal its color and texture. In the country, however, too much light against a black sky will be too great a contrast.

FESTIVE LIGHTS. Lights that bring your nighttime garden to life in celebration of an occasional event or favorite season will lift your spirits and charm your guests. Festive light resources are limited only by your imagination; they include torches, lanterns, luminarias, fire pits, strings of miniature bulbs, floating candles, and inexpensive low-voltage systems that you can set up temporarily and move about for effect as an event or season progresses.

Keep several principles in mind as you consider garden lighting needs:

• Remember that the intensity of light required in a large garden generally decreases as you move away from the house. The reason for this is that our eyes need about ten minutes to completely accommodate to changes in light level when moving from light to dark places. As you step out of the house at night, your eyes won't be adjusted to the darkness and will need more supplemental lighting; as you move outward, your eyes gradually adjust and need less artificial light.

• Take the seasons into consideration. Bathing a distant deciduous tree with light creates one effect in winter and another in midsummer. Attaching a dimmer switch to the light will allow you to adjust its level of brightness and control glare. Installing multiple switches allows you to turn groups of lights off and on as you need them.

• Timers and photocell sensors can be welcome conveniences when attached to task lighting. In particular, they can greatly enhance the effectiveness of security lighting.

• Lights that are not permanently fixed in a single location allow you the flexibility of being able to move fixtures around to reflect different moods and seasonal effects. The technology of low-voltage systems makes this flexibility especially attractive. If you choose permanent fixtures, however, they can be very decorative and functional as well. Fixtures of carved stone in the Japanese style, fixtures of cast metals, and various contemporary fixtures can reinforce your design theme and draw attention to your garden's special points of visual interest. As a general rule, though, I do prefer outdoor lighting that is understated in appearance.

• Good lighting design can never be fully resolved on paper. After working out all the details as best you can in a drawing, I recommend that you do what I do—get the fixtures, invite a qualified electrician (if your project is not extremely simple), select a good night, and *experiment!* It's fun, and you'll be happier with the results.

Furniture and Accessories

FURNITURE AND ACCESSORIES ARE the finishing touches that make your garden complete, visually satisfying, and fully usable.

By necessity, most furniture cannot be placed until your construction is nearly finished. However, I urge you to make selections early and add them to your program as design and construction progresses. Most important, include garden furniture in your budget. It is far too important to appear as an underbudgeted afterthought.

Let me suggest several guidelines for you to keep in mind as you select and place garden furniture and accessories.

• Choose styles, colors, and materials that complement those already used in your house. They should reflect your lifestyle and preferences, and they should be comfortable. There are many materials to choose from—metal, wood, fiberglass, wicker,

carved stone, cast concrete—and each can be fashioned in styles that range from rustic to classical to contemporary. Just remember that contrasting styles may be disconcerting to the eye and diminish the overall unity of your garden's appearance.

• Be inventive. Augment your garden furniture with pieces that don't have to be purchased from a store or custom fabricated. Look around and you may discover unexpected opportunities. Consider, for example, a fixed-in-place seat that extends from a stone wall or a bench at a stair landing where vis-

itors can rest and enjoy the scenery. Look for natural features also: a convenient rock outcropping to serve as a plant stand or a flat boulder that's just the right height for sitting.

• When furnishing outdoor spaces, treat them like indoor rooms. Think about circulation, especially the "door" where you enter the garden room and the circulation patterns that allow you to pass around and through it. Don't place furniture in awkward places, and remember that some pieces require much more space than you imagine. You'll

house—a terrace room or country kitchen, for example—interact visually and functionally with the garden.

• Some garden furniture is wonderfully ornamental and sculptural. Use such pieces to advantage. Placed properly, they will attract the eye and provide moments of visual delight. Some pieces also can be used to frame the view of distant scenery or direct attention to a specimen plant.

be surprised, for example, how much space a couple of chaise longues need, especially when you allow enough space around them for circulation.

• Don't overfurnish your garden. Too much furniture and other extraneous objects lead to a cluttered appearance and take away from the garden's basic visual pleasures.

• Use furniture to strengthen the visual connections between house and garden. Some furniture, for example, can be used either indoors or outside. Placing it in either setting reinforces my notion that the architecture of the house should be pulled into the garden. This concept is especially useful if spaces in your

• If you have a large garden, place a few comfortable chairs or benches in a secluded place. You and your guests will welcome a few moments of respite in a protected nook.

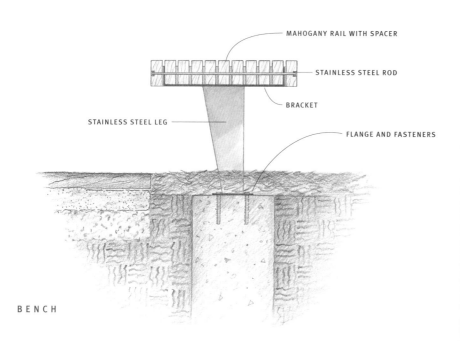

MAHOGANY RAIL WITH SPACER

STAINLESS STEEL ROD

BRACKET

STAINLESS STEEL LEG

FLANGE AND FASTENERS

BENCH

Spiral oak bench at The New Art Garden at Roche Court, Salisbury, England.

• Most garden furniture is easily movable. Moving things about as the garden matures and the seasons change will enhance its ephemeral nature. For larger social functions you almost certainly will want to rearrange and perhaps augment your outdoor furniture. Finally, it's okay to change

things about on a whim; doing so will add to your sense of participation in the garden's evolution.

• Furniture is closely allied with our social instincts. I try to arrange chairs and other items so that they appear to speak to each other.

The Mosaic Garden, Melbourne, Australia.

Works of Fancy

ARBORS, GAZEBOS, PERGOLAS, TREL-
lises—all such open structures make
wonderful additions to the garden, especially when covered with climbing shrubs
or vines. They're like icing on the cake
after the hard work of planning, building,
and planting a garden.

A work of fancy, or what is sometimes rather
unfairly called a "folly," can serve many purposes
other than the obvious one of creating a shady
retreat. It may be the centerpiece of your garden or
the foil that directs a visitor's attention to a piece of
sculpture, a fountain, a specimen plant, or some
other garden attraction. If space is limited, a

gazebo or pergola may be used to imply a greater
depth by directing views to distant attractions.
Alternatively, the work of fancy may be a focal point
itself, catching the visitor's eye while adding a playful dimension to the garden.

As lighthearted as they may be in spirit,
works of fancy can also serve pragmatic purposes.
An arbor, for example, can serve as an extension of

shapes, including rectilinear, curvilinear, or circular, depending on the size and topography of a site. A linear building, such as a pergola, does not have to be continuous—an intermittent or staggered pattern may be preferable, especially if you want to foreshorten a long space. Remember that the top of your garden building does not necessarily have to be flat; a sloped, vaulted, or peaked top will add interest and mini-

your house, providing an outdoor room that is sheltered from the sun. A structure of this kind is the perfect place for benches and garden furniture and provides an ideal spot for entertaining.

I like to take aesthetic risks when I design a garden structure—a fantasy, after all, should soar. Playful garden buildings can take on many

Opposite: Sissinghurst Castle Garden, Kent (the National Trust), England.

mize the "boxcar" look of a linear enclosed space.

A garden building's design should tie the house and garden together. I always begin the design of such structures by studying the house, to identify distinctive colors, materials, and architectural details that can be extended into the garden. The subtle repetition in the work of fancy of cornice details, column

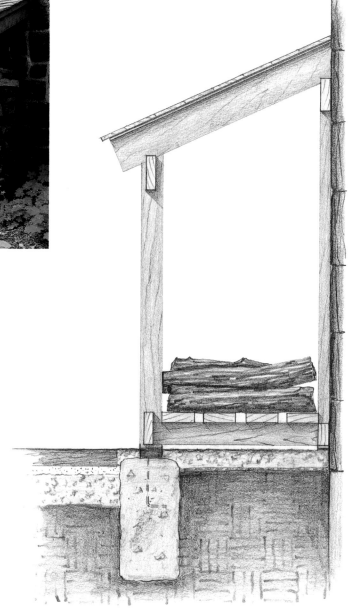

WOOD STORAGE

styles, roof pitches, and other architectural features drawn from the house reinforces the unity
of the composition.

Don't rule out a work of fancy just because
your garden space is limited. An outdoor gallery or
other improvement can be relatively small, and
a structure such as an arbor can even be attached
to your house.

RULES AND REGULATIONS FOR CONSTRUCTION

THROUGHOUT THIS BOOK I HAVE SUGGESTED THAT YOU GET PROFESSIONAL HELP IF YOUR NEW garden plans are anything but very simple, especially if they involve new construction. If nothing else, qualified professionals will help you ensure that what you are planning is consistent with the laws, rules, codes, ordinances, regulations, deed restrictions, and other standards that local jurisdictions use to evaluate construction projects. These requirements aren't merely bureaucratic red tape; they are necessary standards that ensure the structural integrity and safety of your improvements and their compatibility with the surrounding environment.

In most states the codes of the Building Officials and Code Administrators International (BOCA) constitute the basis of rules and regulations. Local officials or your design and engineering professionals will be familiar with the local application of these codes, and they will be able to help you process the necessary permits and approvals.

Be sure to start your garden design process with an accurate survey that shows property boundaries; public rights-of-way; utility and other easements; topography; the "footprints" of permanent buildings; and the location of important site features such as pools, paved surfaces, stairs, walls, fences, and major plant groupings. If you have a septic field it must be shown on the drawing. Accurate and up-to-date survey information is essential for planning, permitting, and construction purposes.

The following is a sample checklist of important matters to look out for as you finalize your garden plans. It's not an exhaustive list—you'll think of others as you proceed—but I hope it will give you a sense of how easy it is to step into murky areas where technical and professional skills are needed. Treat these questions like a test; if the answer to any of them is yes, you probably will need assistance with design, engineering, or permitting.

- Will you need to install new utility services or relocate existing services such as water, gas, electricity, sewers (sanitary or storm), irrigation lines, and communication cables?

- Will you need to clear or grade your property? If so, are protected species of vegetation involved? Will drainage be discharged off-site into waterways or onto neighboring properties? During construction, you may be required to install various types of runoff filters such as fabric or bales of straw.

- Will you be working in or close to environmentally sensitive areas such as wetlands? If so, permits, impact statements, and environmental assessments likely will be required by various governmental jurisdictions.

- Will you be constructing permanent improvements such as retaining walls, fences, steps, decks, railings, or water features? Be aware that they probably are subject to setback, height, and other standards set by local building, zoning, or subdivision codes and that the plans may need to be stamped by licensed professionals for permitting by local authorities.

- Will you be building a swimming pool or other water feature? If so, check local standards for safety and operational requirements related to location, setback, depth, lighting, mechanical and electrical operations, and, especially, protective barriers.

I don't want these procedures to sound too intimidating or onerous, but I do want to emphasize their importance. Once you have satisfied all the requirements, you will have the comfort of knowing that your garden plans are sound and that they are drawn in accordance with established rules and regulations. Also, if you work with technical or professional experts during the permitting and construction process, you will find that their suggestions add to the long-term success of the garden.

Bachelard, Gaston. *The Poetics of Space*. New York: Orion Press, 1964.

Balmori, Diana, Diane Kostial McGuire, and Eleanor M. McPeck. *Beatrix Farrand's American Landscapes*. Sagaponack, N.Y.: Sagapress Inc., 1985.

Bardi, P. M. *The Tropical Gardens of Burle Marx*. New York: Reinhold Publishing Corporation, 1964.

Brookes, John. *The Book of Garden Design*. New York: Macmillan Publishing Company, 1991.

———. *The Small Garden*. London: Marshall Cavendish Books Ltd., 1977.

Brown, Jane. *Beatrix: The Gardening Life of Beatrix Jones Farrand 1872–1959*. New York: Viking, 1995.

———. *Sissinghurst: Portrait of a Garden*. New York: Harry N. Abrams, Inc., 1990.

Church, Thomas D. *Your Private World: A Study of Intimate Gardens*. San Francisco: Chronicle Books, 1969.

———, Grace Hall, and Michael Laurie. *Gardens Are for People*. Berkeley, Calif.: University of California Press, 1995.

Crowe, Sylvia. *Garden Design*. West Sussex & London: Packard Publishing Ltd. in association with Thomas Gibson Publishing, Ltd., 1981.

de collectie sandberg. Amsterdam: J.M. Meulenhoff, 1962.

Francis, Mark, and Randolph T. Hester, Jr. *The Meaning of Gardens: Idea, Place, and Action*. Cambridge, Mass.: The MIT Press, 1990.

Frieze, Charlotte M. *Social Gardens: Outdoor Spaces for Living and Entertaining*. New York: Stewart, Tabori & Chang, Inc., 1988.

Hobhouse, Penelope. *Penelope Hobhouse's Gardening Through the Ages: An Illustrated History of Plants and Their Influence on Garden Styles—from Ancient Egypt to the Present Day*. New York: Simon & Schuster, 1992.

Iwamiya, Takeji, and Teiji Itoh. *Imperial Gardens of Japan*. New York: John Weatherhill, Inc., 1970.

Karson, Robin. *Fletcher Steele, Landscape Architect: An Account of the Gardenmaker's Life, 1888–1971*. New York: Harry N. Abrams, Inc., 1989.

Levy, Leah, and Peter Walker. *Peter Walker: Minimalist Gardens*. Washington, D.C.: Spacemaker Press, 1997.

Lindbergh, Anne Morrow. *Gift from the Sea*. New York: Vintage Books, 1991.

Littlefield, Susan S. H. *Seaside Gardening: Plantings, Procedures, and Design Principles*. New York: Simon & Schuster, Inc., 1986.

Masson, Georgina. *Italian Gardens*. New York: Harry N. Abrams, Inc., 1961.

Meyer, Elizabeth K. *Martha Schwartz: Transfiguration of the Commonplace*. Washington, D.C.: Spacemaker Press, 1997.

Moore, Charles W., William J. Mitchell, and William Turnbull, Jr. *Poetics of Gardens*. Cambridge, Mass.: The MIT Press, 1988.

Mosser, Monique, and Georges Teyssot. *The Architecture of Western Gardens: A Design History from the Renaissance to the Present Day*. Cambridge, Mass.: The MIT Press, 1990.

Oehme, Wolfgang, James van Sweden, and Susan Rademacher Frey, rev. *Bold Romantic Gardens*. Washington, D.C.: Spacemaker Press, 1998.

Page, Russell. *The Education of a Gardener*. New York: Random House, 1983.

Pereire, Anita, and Gabrielle van Zuylen. *Gardens of France*. New York: Harmony Books, 1983.

"Peter Walker William Johnson and Partners: Art and Nature." *Process Architecture*, June, 1994, No. 118.

Rogers, Elizabeth Barlow. *Landscape Design: A Cultural and Architectural History.* New York: Harry N. Abrams, Inc., 2001.

Rose, James C. *Creative Gardens.* New York: Reinhold Publishing Corporation, 1958.

van Sweden, James. *Gardening with Nature.* New York: Random House, Inc., 1997.

———. *Gardening with Water.* New York: Random House, Inc., 1995.

Verey, Rosemary. *Classic Garden Design: How to Adapt and Recreate Garden Features of the Past.* New York: Congdon & Weed, 1984.

Waldman, Diane. *Willem de Kooning.* New York: Harry N. Abrams, Inc., 1988.

Wilkinson, Elizabeth, and Marjorie Henderson. *The House of Boughs: A Sourcebook of Garden Designs, Structures, and Suppliers.* New York: Viking Penguin, Inc., 1985.

Design participants with OEHME, VAN SWEDEN & ASSOCIATES

THE DIAMOND GARDEN
Shope Reno Wharton Associates, Architects

A GARDEN BY THE SHORE
Shope Reno Wharton Associates, Architects

AN ISLAND RETREAT
William McDonough, Architects

THE MINTZ GARDEN
Michael Hauptman, Brawer & Hauptman, Architects

A NEW WORLD COTTAGE
Franklin Salasky, B Five Studio, Architects

SHORT POINT FARM
Mary Meagher, Mary Meagher Design, Architects

THE SULLIVAN GARDEN
David Jones Architects

DESIGNERS

Michael Balston 208
John Brookes 186 (bottom), 213 (top)
Alison Crowther 245 (top)
Maria de Haan 240 (bottom)
Topher Delaney 216 (top), 233, 234 (bottom)
Bradley Dyruff 219 (bottom)
Beatrix Farrand 211 (bottom), 213 (bottom), 220
Isabelle Greene 216 (bottom)
Tessa Hobbs 196 (top)
Penelope Hobhouse 217
Edith Julien 212 (top)
Raymond Jungles 222 (bottom), 228 (top), 240 (top)
Michel Langevin 212 (top)
Christopher Lloyd 178
Sir Edwin Luytens 212 (bottom)
Roberto Burle Marx 195, 223 (top)
Keeyla Meadows 245 (center)
Rob W. Mc Farland, Ward & Child \ The Garden Store 231 (bottom)
Melani Mignault 212 (top)
Alfonso Ossorio 184 (top), 199 (top)
Martin Puryear 186 (top)
Diana Ridell 190 (top)
Richard Schultz 245 (bottom)

Miles Warren 187 (center)
Faith and George Whitten 201 (bottom)
Debra Yates (ceramic murals) 222 (bottom), 240 (top)
Zion & Breen Associates 89

ILLUSTRATORS

Ching-Fang Chen 52, 53 (bottom), 57, 58, 64, 74, 100, 105, 116, 138, 144, 150 (bottom), 152, 172, 224, 241, 244
Sophie Larrimore 150 (top), 183, 188, 198, 204
James van Sweden 4
Tetsuya Yamamoto 53 (top), 54, 59, 60, 63, 75, 77, 83, 88, 141, 157, 160, 161, 210, 252

PHOTOGRAPHERS

James van Sweden *unless otherwise noted*

Steve Ahlgren 90, 92
Yalcin Erhan 233, 234 (bottom)
Richard Felber iv, 44, 50, 54, 55, 56, 59, 61, 65, 72, 76, 79, 84, 85, 95, 140, 141, 143, 144, 145, 146, 148, 149, 151, 153, 174, 175, 176, 181 (bottom), 182 (bottom), 183 (top), 202 (bottom), 203, 205 (top), 206, 209, 214 (top), 215 (top), 225, 230, 231 (top), 232, 246, 248, 249, 252
Roger Foley 80, 82, 98, 108, 111, 112, 114, 117, 118, 120, 121 (bottom), 122, 124, 125, 126, 127, 128, 129, 179, 181 (top and center), 189 (top), 197, 205 (bottom), 211, 213 (bottom), 219 (top), 220, 226, 239, 247 (top)
Mick Hales 192 (top), 195, 196 (bottom), 242
Jerry Harpur 96, 134, 142, 154, 160, 170, 173, 186 (bottom), 196 (top), 200 (bottom), 201 (bottom), 208, 212 (top), 216, 217, 219 (bottom), 245 (center), 250
Alice Hoachlander 87
Raymond Jungles 228 (top), 240 (top)
Andrew Lawson 28, 187 (center), 190 (top), 199 (bottom), 200 (top), 201 (top), 202 (top), 218, 245 (top), 247 (bottom), 251
John Neubauer 235, 237
Pamela Palmer 12
Lanny Provo 222 (bottom)
Martha Schwartz 10
John Sims 6
Alan Ward 89

Index

Page numbers in *italics* refer to illustrations.

Following training as an architect and landscape architect in the United States and the Netherlands, J A M E S VA N S W E D E N 's early practice led to a 1977 partnership with landscape architect and horticulturist Wolfgang Oehme. A revolutionary garden style quickly emerged and continues to flourish.

Mr. van Sweden's designs draw attention first to dramatic spectacles of informal planting and then to the practical beauty of architectural "bones" that anchor his gardens to the ground. The garden's underlying architecture is the subject of this book.

By revealing the secrets of his unusual design approach, Mr. van Sweden's recent books, *Gardening with Water* and *Gardening with Nature*, have inspired professional and amateur gardeners alike. His first book, *Bold Romantic Gardens*, co-authored with Mr. Oehme, is also considered a classic in the field.

Mr. van Sweden is a Fellow of the American Society of Landscape Architects and recipient of many distinguished awards. His works are published widely in gardening books and periodicals, and he is a frequent guest on television and radio shows. He lives in Washington, D.C.